# STICKIN' IT TO THE MATRIX

## DEAN HENDERSON

*For my mother, Jeanette, who taught me to Work and to Save and for my grandmother, Marguerite, who taught me to Live Simply.*

# CONTENTS

Preface

Copyright

Dedication

Chapter 1: Love the People, Hate the System

Chapter 2: Get Out of Debt

Chapter 3: Housing

Chapter 4: Transportation

Chapter 5: Food, Clothing & Bills

Chapter 6: Mercenary Shopping

Chapter 7: Sell More Than You Buy

Chapter 8: The Grubstake

Chapter 9: The Power of Compound Interest

Chapter 10: Get Back to the Garden

About the Author

Other Books by Dean Henderson

# PREFACE

This will likely not be the last book I write, because this is the final of four things that I have to say about my experience living in this world that I deem important enough to go to the trouble of writing a book about.

My first book, *Big Oil & Their Bankers in the Persian Gulf: Four Horsemen, Eight Families & Their Global Intelligence, Narcotics & Terror Network*, draws a diagram connecting the various tentacles of the bad guys who condescendingly call themselves the *Illuminati* and who lord over this planet via their central banking/oil/weapons/drugs oligopoly.

I spent 14 years researching this way-stranger-than-fiction book, which began as a Master's thesis. Chapter 19: *The Eight Families* was recently published in German language as my third book under the title *Das Kartell der Federal Reserve*.

Matrix agents - probably named Smith - have tried to kill me twice because of *Big Oil...* It contains every single thing I know about these assholes. But here I am.

As Morpheus said, "We must lose all fear."

Fear provides the foundation which underpins the matrix. In its absence, the matrix will collapse.

As Crazy Horse said, "It's a good day to die". He didn't mean he wanted to die. He meant he wanted to live every day without fear or the regret that stems from that fear. This way if he should die, it would be a good day to die.

I could have cowered and went away after those two attempts on my life - one in New Mexico and one on the Zimbabwe/South Africa border. But I didn't. I got louder, wrote more and became more defiant of these scumbags.

If I can live without fear after what they tried to do to me, surely you can lose your fear of the matrix. Come on man!

Besides, in baseball, 0-2 translates into the very lousy batting average of .000. Lesson one, never overestimate the matrix. In general, it is lethargic, stupid and overconfident.

My second book, *The Grateful Unrich: Revolution in 50 Countries*, chronicles my *real* education during my shoestring travels to 50 foreign countries, some many times over.

I learned much more from these escapades than I ever did earning my MS, though I came away with many valuable things from going to college as well.

Everyone should travel. And everyone should experience college, even if you end up using the useless peace of paper you'll get - as I did - for other more pressing matters in life.

I started that second book at age 21. I finished at age 45. The title is another double entendre, same as with the first book. *"Big Oil & Their Bankers in the Persian Gulf"* could imply coziness between what I coin the Four Horsemen of oil and the international bankers like JP Morgan Chase, et al. Or it could refer to Four Horsemen collusion with Kuwait, Saudi Arabia and other "banker" Persian Gulf despot regimes who keep the world economy afloat via their regular purchases of 30-Year US Treasury bonds.

In the case of the second book, I humbly borrow the phrase "the grateful unrich" from my fellow Show Me Stater and hero Samuel Clemons, who, after his years piloting riverboats up and down the Mighty Mississippi, adopted the pen name Mark Twain.

In one of his more obscure texts, Twain used that phrase to describe what could also be called "the climbers" – those of firmly lower and middle class means who spend their days fawning at the feet of the rich, gladly licking their fascist boots, though they themselves barely have a pot to piss in.

In the case of *The Grateful Unrich...,* this phrase also has a double meaning. As I've wandered the world I have persistently witnessed the supposedly backpacker-cool sons and daughters of these Twain-described Western losers treat local people in the developing world worse than a southern slave owner would treat a servant.

Simultaneously, I have encountered time and again the incredible kindness and humanity emanating from my local hosts, whose attitude completes the double entendre, as they are also the "grateful unrich".

This fourth book, *Stickin' it to the Matrix*, springs out of the same experiences which culminated in the writing of these previous books.

I've witnessed first hand the carnage which the *Illuminati* thugs and their enabling "grateful unrich" muses continue to inflict upon the global poor and the planet itself. Since then I've tracked down their corporate interlocks and their banking pyramids, studied their penchant for human sacrifice and little boys, puzzled over their arrogance in treating us like *goyim* (cattle), and revealed their NAMES. That's what put me on their "greatest hits" list.

Fuck em'!

Out of this roller-coaster-ride awakening comes *Stickin' it to the Matrix*, which I hope will serve as practical guide on how to escape the matrix.

In the spirit of keeping things simple - a lesson I learned from my grandma Marguerite and a central theme of this text - this book will be much shorter and to the point.

My hope is that this how-to-guide will spring you from your nine-to-five wage slavery cubical and set you along the path of liberation and emancipation from the matrix.

The main task at hand is to deprogram readers from the consumer shopping mall mindset hell that most of the world has unhappily settled upon. Beyond that, I hope you will take away a new audacity *towards* the matrix.

While these four books may seem entirely unrelated, if you take a deeper look you will see that they are in fact inextricably linked.

Still, in a world where most authors only wish to become famous and or to make money by recycling the same boring information over and over under different book titles, I have stubbornly chosen what I consider to be the more honorable path of writing books on different topics in disparate genres.

Most authors want to become known as "experts" in their field. I despise the very notion of "experts". In fact I think the entire concept of "experts" is a fraud used by the *Illuminati* to keep us pinned within their top-down authoritarian pyramid. Nor do I have time for "masters", "sirs", "lords" or self-important charlatans by any other name.

Once I studied and internalized how evil the matrix agenda truly is, then traveled to villages where children were not getting even one meal in a day, I made the quite obvious link between starving children and matrix banker/corporate crimes.

From that point on my soul has found it necessary for my physical being to reside as far away from this rotten and rigged system as possible. I call it nonparticipation. This book chronicles the methods I have used to create such separation.

But I believe in both dropping out of the matrix *and* being a political activist. Why choose only one path, when you can be happier integrating the two into an even better path. Probably it's because the matrix told you to think this way.

Much of what is required for emancipation from the matrix is *unlearning* all the mumbo jumbo garbage you've been fed since you were just out of diapers.

So in the spirit of defiance, *Stickin' it to the Matrix* goes one step beyond nonparticipation in the matrix and gives some pointers on how you can actually *extract* many free things you need from this rotten system which has thrived for a few centuries on the daily exploitation of the people and the planet.

If you can turn this creed into a lifestyle, you will not only be emancipating *yourself* from the matrix, you will be - much more importantly - helping all living beings out by striving to destroy their matrix prison cell as well.

No justice. No peace. Revolution is the only solution!

I come from a working class farm family and was never handed anything. I've earned every dime I've saved over the years.

The longest "real job" I ever had lasted five months. The last was in 1993. Though always at the margins, from the age of 28, I completely exited the job market and began steering my own ship. I "retired" from the matrix and I've never looked back.

If you enjoy working for some asshole boss, suffer from Stockholm Syndrome (constantly trying to curry favor from your oppressor), get a kick out of being surrounded by idiots all day, love your yearly company Christmas Party, or if you are the loudest person singing your company song in the morning, this book is not for you. You need therapy.

If you've bought into the popular matrix sitcom rerun that "the one who dies with the most toys wins" or enjoy burning as much gas as possible in a Hummer while running over small creatures, or make a living screwing over your friends and family, you're an asshole.

But if you feel like telling your boss where it stick it, unleashing your fury on a water cooler and expeditiously exiting the well-trodden path of miserable indentured servitude - which keeps the bad guys in the saddle and you their penned sheeple - I hope this book can launch you down the road to freedom, emancipation and liberation.

I hope that you will soon plug into the revolutionary collective consciousness of planet earth, embrace everyday audacity in your dealings with the system and start *Stickin it to the Matrix*.

Chapter 1

# Love the People, Hate the System

The key to getting free from the matrix is attitude. Every day we are bombarded with a not so subtle message from the programmers. They want you to hate the people and the planet starting with yourself.

You smell bad; therefore you need matrix-manufactured aluminum-laden deodorant. Your teeth aren't white enough; therefore you buy tooth-rotting fluoride toothpaste from our subsidiary in the Cayman Islands. You're too fat; therefore you need the matrix diabetes river diet plan. And so on.

You should also know that these illuminated bloodline lizard chosen ones want to kill you, so their inbred children will have more space to roam and exploit the planet.

Every "program" on your TV degrades your humanity by telling you to screw over your friends and neighbors and "get one over on them". The not so subtle message in all of this is to "be a good capitalist".

Most news stories on your local news are about poor people committing crimes. White collar criminals such as the financial parasites who own Wall Street are not so covered. That's because these criminals own the system, including the TV station you are watching, which is indeed programming you.

If the rich can keep you focused on all those poor liquor store bandits and the Octomom, they can continue to feed incessantly at the government trough, all the while robbing billions through their systematic insider trading on the global stock exchanges. And the much more serious crimes of these pedophile maniacs will go unnoticed.

The broken record which they try to engrain in each of their slaves from birth is essentially, "You are inherently flawed (original sin), but the system itself is perfect. You are a basket case, but the matrix has no flaws. Hate yourself and worship the system, along with the oligarchy that owns it".

Once you begin to see that the system is actually predicated on exploitation, cheating and lies, you can do one of two things. You can choose to embrace the system and become morally bankrupt yourself by working to further the goals of an evil corporation, investing your retirement in their rigged stock markets and hoping in vain that the matrix, by getting yet more sinister and more powerful will somehow benefit you.

A rising tide may well lift all boats, but how exactly this translates into a phony bunch of paunchy overpaid bankers lording over us is a bit of a stretch. These bastards would grab the first life rafts from any sinking ship and gladly leave you to die.

Ditto their oft-repeated "survival of the fittest" Charles Darwin-the-Freemason mantra. Do you really think these old button-pushing yachter fucks own their global central banking money-printing oligopoly because they are more *fit* than you or I? If so, I've got some well-priced swamp land in Florida you really need to take a look at.

Programming is a bitch.

The other and healthier choice you can make once you realize the books are cooked by the cannibals, is to become thoroughly disillusioned – not a bad thing at all since this oft-maligned word implies that you have merely lost your previously off-the-mark illusions about Santa Claus, the tooth ferry and the Rothschild lizard kings.

Denial is another major girder of the matrix, which relies on mass cognitive dissonance to disseminate its lies. It is much healthier to face hard facts which counter this onslaught of propaganda, much as you would be wise to do should, say, a grizzly bear attack you.

In this dire scenario, should you opt to hold your hands over your ears and wish the grizzly bear away, you will be eaten. It's no different when dealing with the *Illuminati*, save for the fact that this much more nefarious ilk, left unchecked, will gladly dine on your children and grandchildren in perpetuity.

The irony is that in opening your eyes widely and taking in all of the heinous acts that constitute the matrix, you will embrace truth. In this moment you will also embrace your humanity. And at that tipping point there is only one choice.

You must distance yourself from the system through nonparticipation, begin to construct your own more just systems and go to war with the matrix every day and in every facet of your life. You must make it the central purpose of your life.

The two most effective ways to fight this battle are to withhold your own sweat in the form of cheap labor for the exploiters and to tightly close your pocketbook on its big box stores.

The old saying, "Live simply so that others may simply live", holds true. Your cheap labor and your high-dollar shopping only serve to reinforce the matrix and its global sweatshop plantation.

I will not further chronicle the evils of the matrix in this book. All the evidence you need that this world is run by a group calling itself the *Illuminati*, and which profits from death, destruction and debt is documented in my *Big Oil...*book.

Stories of how our rampant consumption of these Satanists' products in the developed world literally starves out what these creeps call the "useless eaters" of the developing world can be abundantly found in my *The Grateful Unrich...* book.

My task herein is not to convince you that this system is rotten to the core or that you *should* practice non-participation as a way to both emancipate yourself and the rest of the planet from these takers.

My task is to show you in simple and practical terms, *how* to do it. This book will only be of help to those of you who already know what should be obvious to any sentient being who has witnessed oligarchy atrocities, and who wish to begin practicing their political beliefs in their daily lives.

Before one can take action to escape the matrix, one must become a warrior in the battle against it. From that point on one realizes that distancing oneself from the system as much as possible requires a worldview which loves the people and deems the system our enemy.

If you worship the system, or even see it as a valid alternative, you will begin to lose your humanity. You will become cynical as to the motives of your fellow humans and doubtful of natural law. Paradoxically, if you love humanity and the natural world, you must hate the system with all of your heart. You must declare war on it.

This paradox has rewards, which can be viewed from either a spiritual perspective, which a *sanyasi* would call "instant karma", or from a scientific viewpoint commonly known as "every action produces an equal and opposite reaction". In the end, these two are the exact same thing.

So while it may seem that "declaring war on the system" would be an arduous and difficult path, what you will find is that – due to the two abovementioned truisms – once you have embarked upon this road, life actually gets much easier and more enjoyable.

Liberation is attained through empathy for all of life. My old friend Wayne enunciated this important principle best as simply, "Love of Life".

Fighting off the constant advances of the matrix becomes a game. Defending the people from their destruction becomes paramount. And it's lots of fun.

Your heart becomes light again. Stress is alleviated. Time moves more slowly with the pace of nature, instead of at the conjured breakneck speed of the matrix – which is designed to disorient us, confuse us and deny us knowledge of who we really are and why we are here.

This is not to say that the transition will be without difficulty. The matrix is designed so that every citizen within its grasp is commissioned with a thought police badge.

Once you embark upon the path of liberation you will encounter family, friends and neighbors who will attempt to police you back into the matrix in a variety of ways. They will not even realize that they are doing it. It is fear, plain and simple.

They don't want you to leave them behind in the system but don't have the courage to come along, so they will make constant attempts to drag you back into the swamp of misery in which they reside. Their own unhappiness will be the basis through which they attempt to ostracize, mock and isolate you back into the flock.

They are the main policing mechanism on which the matrix relies to keep you in prison. So you must be resolute, brave and strong. Don't take it personally. And realize that they are not bad people, they are just scared.

Once you have endured this societal ridicule and made it safely to higher ground, you can then reach back into the muck and help your friends and family escape its grasp as well.

You must also realize that most will never grab your hand for a lift out. Creature comforts and intense matrix propaganda have trapped them in an illusion of happiness.

Many are still stuck in the nonsense of trying to gain acceptance from their parents, their neighbors or the town folk. This guilt/shame driven phenomenon keeps more people trapped in the matrix than any other. Love your parents; don't live trying to please them.

But some people will grab your hand and climb out. In my life there have been many. This is very gratifying and reaffirms the path of liberation and collective consciousness.

There will be loneliness on this barely traveled road. The majority of people will never really "get it". This must be accepted as the price of freedom. But it is a price that is well worth paying.

As you get further down the path of liberation from the matrix, you will meet a growing number of others who are heading in the same positive direction. And many of these kindred spirits will become your very best friends.

Chapter 2

# Get Out of Debt

The first thing that you need to do in order to get on the road to freedom is to get completely out of debt. The main fodder off of which the matrix feeds worldwide and at every level – personal, governmental and business – is debt. If they can keep us collectively chained to their phony fiat currency scheme, they can keep us quiet and subservient to their will.

The first debt to get rid of is ALL credit card debt. The interest rates that the Visa/Master Card Cartel charges are exorbitant. And they are owned largely by two of the biggest *Illuminati*-controlled banks on earth – JP Morgan Chase and Citigroup. Our destiny on this earth is certainly not to feed vampires.

Once you pay off all your credit card debt, don't ever go there again. Cancel and cut up all credit cards but one, as sometimes one is needed to rent a car or some other thing. I keep an airline-miles-earning Visa due to its international accessibility.

NEVER use even this one card except for things like car rental which, unfortunately still usually requires a credit card. On the infrequent occasion that you do use it, make sure to pay the balance off by the deadline that month to avoid usurious interest charges.

No wage slave dare openly speak ill of his/her boss or of the system in general, lest they risk being fired. Without a job how can they then make their house payment, car payment and so on? Because of their debt load, many Americans – even the well-paid ones – are just one paycheck away from living on the streets.

While paying off credit card debt may seem a daunting task to those of you who are buried in the stuff, it is essential to escaping the matrix. If you are able to nothing else in this book, get out of credit card debt.

There's a saying I heard once that made a whole lot of sense to me. "Live like no one lives now and you'll live like no one lives later".

The implication is to live not only within your means, but below your means. Once you begin to do this you can not only easily erase your credit card debt, you can start to save money.

Start a bank account with a small community bank if you don't have one already. These are not evil institutions and should never be seen in the same light as the *Illuminati* mafia.

In fact these small banks are an integral part of any town since they finance businesses, housing, etc. One thing you will learn while exiting the matrix is how important it is to lose your dogma on a range of issues and make moral decisions based on reality rather than somebody else's accepted theory of the day.

There are different kinds of bankers, different kinds of politicians, different kinds of business people, loggers, hunters, lawyers, etc. Some own the matrix, some sell out to it, and some work against it. That is reality. Trade in your dogma for some karma.

Starting a bank account protects you from acting impulsively in accordance with the nonstop matrix shopping program. It's much easier to spend money you are carrying on your person or have sitting in a drawer at home. Keeping your money in a bank makes it harder for you to spend it and watching it grow will encourage you to continue working towards your freedom.

Significantly, when you've paid off your debt and you start a savings or checking account, you cease to be a debtor to the bankers and begin to be their creditor. That savings account you started is a loan to the bank which they then lend out at a higher interest rate. As such, the banker is required to pay you interest on that loan which, while currently miniscule and pathetic, fluctuates according to the prime rate set by the Federal Reserve cartel.

Go to a system of paying CASH for everything. If you write lots of checks or use a debit card too much, it's easy to lose track of your account balance.

I had significant debt only twice in my life. Once I took out around $5,000 in student loans to get my Bachelor's Degree. The second time we had a $10,000 mortgage on the first property we owned.

Both times these debts were paid off within a year. The key was most definitely living below my means. The other key was working all the overtime I could get at the various jobs I had.

My father died when I was 12 years old in a car accident. We operated a farm at the time. I loved playing baseball in the summer and was a pretty good catcher and lead-off hitter, but with Dad gone money got tight, we had to sell the farm place and my Mom lined me up with my first job for a local farmer. The pay was $2.25/hour.

I learned to operate all types of farm equipment and soon found a job for $3.00/hour, then one for $4.00/hour. As farmers in the area began hearing stories of what a hard worker I was and how competent I was at operating machinery, they competed to have me work for them in the summers. At the end of my "farming phase" I was making $6.00/hour and working 60-70 hours a week. I missed playing baseball, but racked up around $4,000 in savings.

In those days interest rates were high and Mom wisely got me invested in a certificate of deposit (CD) that paid 13% interest. So when I went off to college, I had a little cushion and didn't have to take out as many student loans as some kids.

Even so, I worked my way through college at various pizza joints (lots of free food), libraries and work study jobs. My senior year of college I worked three different jobs at once. And when I graduated I had a job lined up as a fly fishing guide on the Alaskan Peninsula that paid very well. Room and board was included and since we were in the middle of nowhere, there was nothing to spend my paychecks on.

Due to all that hard work, my student loans were paid off and I was able to save enough money for a two-month overland backpacking trip to Mexico, Belize and Guatemala. I was completely out of debt and seeing the world at age 22.

The first leg of that journey south was driven from Omaha to McAllen, TX on the Mexican border in an auto driveaway car.

These companies still exist and this is an excellent way to travel for free.

Usually someone has driven their car somewhere and due to some unexpected contingency they have to fly home. Your role is to get their car back to them. Gas and insurance are paid, so the ride is free. Google "auto driveaway" and find out if you have one near you.

The second time I was in debt was when we bought our first property – 10 acres and a beat up mobile home. By that time I was 27 years old, had my Master's Degree, had traveled solo around the world and was married to my beautiful wife, Jill.

In my travels, the lessons in simple living that my parents and grandparents had instilled in me on the farm sunk in even deeper. We send out the Peace Corps to condescendingly "teach" the developing world how to live, while *Illuminati* corporations and banks plunder their resources. Ironically, I have learned so much about how to live *from* the global poor.

But you can see the same thing here in the US, if you look.

Mexicans come here to work the hard jobs that Americans won't. They cram as many workers as they can into beat up mobile homes to save on rent. Nearly every dime they earn is then sent back to their families in Mexico who are socking that money away into savings accounts so that these hard-working wanderers can eventually go home and retire to a nice country home.

Don't let appearances fool you. The Mexicans keeping those Des Moines meat packing plants humming are far more wealthy that most Americans. They are creditors.

When I got my MS in 1991, I was totally broke. So I lined up another good paying job, this time in Japan teaching English. They flew me over in Business Class, where I filled my luggage with as many free tiny bottles of Jack Daniels as I could coax out of the stewardess. They also gave us a free house to live in and car. In only five months our bank account went from $0 to $15,000. It was our first grubstake.

From Kobe, we hopped a ferry to Shanghai, China and spent three months visiting China, Macao, Hong Kong, Thailand,

Malaysia, the Philippines and Hawaii. We were creditors again and seeing the world.

We spent $4,000 traveling and buying a car at an LA auction when we returned, so we rolled into the Ozarks in the fall of 1992 with a 1965 Plymouth Reliant packed to the gills. Our two dogs – Buck and Milo – had to sit atop our stuff in the back seat.

After a night sleeping in that packed car, we saw an ad for 10 acres and a mobile home for $29,900. We had a look, offered them $20,000 and moved in that night.

We put $10,000 down and signed a five-year contact for deed. When the dust had settled and the propane tank was filled, we had only a couple hundred dollars left to our name.

The only answer was to hit the ground running. I worked a variety of temporary agency jobs assembling BB guns, packing baby wipes and whatever, while Jill landed a job at a radio station. We had to borrow $4,000 from her parents to buy Jill a reliable pickup to drive to work.

Within two months I landed a job as a drill crew roustabout on a dam repair project. At $7.00/hour it was the best paying job in the depressed Ozarks. I worked 70 hours a week, taking all the overtime I could get.

During this time, I "borrowed" a copy of Abbie Hoffman's *Steal This Book* from a public library which wishes to remain anonymous. For those of you who have read it, hopefully you will not wonder why I thought about calling this book, *Steal This Book... Again*. I learned many things from that excellent book.

Within days of finishing it, a hillbilly named John who worked at the dam, smoked massive quantities of weed and had a beard down to his knees, "borrowed" it from me. I never saw it again.

Meanwhile we were eating copious amounts of macaroni and cheese and fried bologna, dumpster-diving furniture and growing a massive garden.

One day I went in to pay the monthly house note of $250. I asked the realtor to confirm what we still owed and was shocked to learn of the word "amortization".

For those as naïve as I was, this nasty word means that when you start to pay down a house loan, you pay far more interest than principal. As such, we owed the realtor far more than we thought we did.

Armed with this new and depressing knowledge, we hatched a plan. Jill had already quit her job at the radio station. She could no longer take the lies required to sell advertising, nor the depths that her coworkers would sink to "sell air".

We sold the pickup we had bought for her. Because we had done our research and purchased it from a private individual, we had bought the pickup for the below-book price of $4,000. We sold it for the book value price of $4,600.

We paid back her folks, then took every dime of the rest of our savings and made a lump-sum payment of $7,000 towards the property. That done, the remaining house payments would go mostly towards principle.

Within eleven months of moving in, we paid the place off. When I went in to make the final $250 payment, the realtor was so floored at our determination that he refused to take that last check. Instead, he gave us the deed and we owned our place free and clear.

We had joked all along that they never would have sold that place to us for that price, but for the fact that they figured they'd be repossessing it a few months after we could no longer make the payments. We must have been quite the site when we rolled into their office in that packed-to-the-gills 65' Plymouth.

We were out of debt and worn out from the grind, so we decided to rent the place out for $275/month, bought a 1978 Chevy van for $500, built a bed in it out of scrap lumber and hit the road.

A little over a year later we sold that place for $26,000. We hadn't made much of a profit, but had lived rent free for a year and made some rental income the next year, which we spent living rent-free in that Chevy van.

More importantly, since we had the place paid off, we were able to put every penny of that $26,000 into a savings account. At age 28, we had just taken a quantum leap on the road to freedom. It changed everything.

To summarize, there are two simple keys to getting out of debt. First, work long hours and keep looking for the best paying job around even as you work a less desirable job.

Don't settle into some low-paying job because it's easy. Laziness is the surest way to a life of slavery. This is why the matrix is constantly sending us signals that laziness is somehow a virtue. The mantra goes that you should attempt to get by with as little effort as possible, that you are getting one over on the system by being lazy.

Like all matrix propaganda, nothing could be further from the truth. Be industrious and work hard for your freedom.

Second, you must scrimp and scrape and live below your means. Turn down the heat in winter and use blankets, open the windows in the summer, don't buy anything you don't absolutely need and sell things you have that you don't need. Be proactive. It's your life.

And remember, if you live like no one lives now, you will live like no one lives later.

Chapter 3

# Housing

A big part of living like no one lives now is to reject sedentary living early and often. Being nomadic gives you a chance to see different parts of this amazing world, while inculcating a healthy diligence towards the unnecessary and corrosive accumulation of "stuff".

Historically, humans have not lived sedentary lives. Indigenous peoples were all either nomadic or semi-nomadic. Sedentary living emerged with the rise of modern agriculture.

Many an anthropological scholar has wrestled with the question as to why humans abandoned their relatively easy lives as hunters and gatherers and settled into lives as sedentary agriculturalists. Many scholars of the Sumerian clay tablets – the oldest written language known to man – are now arguing that this sudden transition to agricultural existence may have been *forced* upon humans by the *Illuminati* predecessor – and possibly blood relative – Annunaki space visitors from the distressed planet of Nubira. Interesting stuff!

A huge component of the matrix programmers' master plan for keeping you a wage/debt slave is via shopping and material possessions. If you live in a big house, there's lots of room to put all manner of needless possessions in it. God forbid your colossal house look empty.

How many people do you know who are living in a huge McMansion they hate, mired in debt, who refuse to entertain the option of moving on based on the burgeoning number of plastic storage bins appearing in their crammed garage?

Stuff keeps you staked to the ground like a tethered goat. The more you get, the less money you save, the more debt you grow, the more tied you are to a "job".

The lack of mobility this creates cripples countless humans to a life of boredom and sameness. More importantly, it denies them the economic opportunities that arise with increased mobility. The biggest of these opportunities is in the arena of housing.

The first rule is to live in a small house. The one I live in now feels spacious and measures at 750 square feet. There's less to clean, you have to pay for less energy, and it fosters the notion of simple living and brings a sense of humility to your existence.

As the Lakota proverb goes, "We are not much, but we are a whole lot more than nothing".

Whether you rent or are buying your place on time, housing payments consume the majority of most people's income.

The second rule is that the quicker you can own your house free and clear, the quicker your life will take a huge change for the better.

Everyone not born to money must rent for awhile to gather a down payment on property. Look for places that pay utilities as they can be better deals, especially with recent surges in electricity and other utility costs. With the recent downturn in the economy monthly hotels are sprouting up across the US.

These can be great deals because all bills are paid *and* the place is furnished, allowing you to sell furniture and other possessions before you move in, and to be more mobile on the way out when you will need to be mobile to find that place to buy.

If you're single, better yet are flop houses or rooms in someone else's house where you share a kitchen and bath. Rent is cheap, they too are often furnished and the bills are usually paid. I stayed in a series of these places before I was married.

You meet some very interesting people at these places too. One place I stayed at in Brookings, SD while attending college was full of Arabic-speaking agricultural engineering students from throughout the Middle East.

After we banked that $26,000 from our first "back-to-the-land" attempt, things were never the same. We bought and fixed up a few more properties, making money every time we sold.

In each case we spent hardly any money fixing the places up. Instead we used lots of elbow grease or "sweat equity", as the bankers call it. Except there was no need to build "equity", as after that first place, we always bought our houses with cash.

The first place was another trailer in a park where everyone owned their own lot. We spent $20,000 and sold it for $21,000. Yet we put hardly a dime into it and saved paying rent or a house note for those two years.

In 2001 as our dogs aged we knew we had to get back to the country to give them a peaceful place to pass on. Using the internet we found a place back in the Ozarks. It was a nice smaller 2 BR house on 20 Acres near Peace Valley, MO with an asking price of $59,900.

After we finally sold our house we loaded our $500 81' Chevy Van and headed south. The day we arrived we discovered the place was going up for auction the next day. We were the only bidders and got the place for $49,900 cash.

In 2005 I saw the housing bust looming. So we had the prerequisite yard sales – which yielded $3000 in road cash – and put the place up for sale. Our boys had both passed peacefully and were able to live out there lives in a quiet country setting.

Yes, it was a bit difficult to leave our boys buried there and move on, but my understanding is that they came right along with us anyway.

Through lots of hard work – with no boss but ourselves – we had turned that place into a parked out garden paradise. We sold it for $117,500. After commissions for realtors and closing costs were paid we pocketed $60,000.

With that grubstake banked, we were one giant step closer to living our dream.

Because we lived there longer than two years owner-occupied, we were again exempt from owing any capital gains tax. This two-year time period is key to making money when buying, improving and selling real estate because this exemption is significant.

It also discourages "flipping", which I believe to be immoral. When investing in housing, one should earn their money through honest hard work and improvements, not through laziness and sheer speculation. Otherwise you're simply reinforcing the matrix paradigm.

Traveling light, we again hit the road, this time vagabonding through Panama, Costa Rica, Thailand, Cambodia, Vietnam, Laos, Malaysia, Indonesia, Singapore, Australia and New Zealand.

When we returned to the Ozarks we knew the housing bust had only just begun, so rather than trading up, as many people look to do, we were looking to trade down.

We found a small older 1 BR house on 3 acres just two miles from Greer Spring and the National Scenic Eleven Point River and near the town of Alton, MO. Asking price was $49,900 completely furnished. We offered $40,000 and the seller refused. We let it sit awhile. Two weeks later we offered him $41,500 and he accepted.

We dug our gardens, planted fruit and net trees, landscaped with perennials, put in a new lagoon with the help of a backhoe and fixed the house some – mainly cosmetics.

When buying a house look for the proverbial diamond in the rough. The perfect example is a house that needs a paint job or sits on an overgrown lot or has junk strewn all over the yard, but IS STRUCTURALLY SOLID!

Remember that houses which have sat on the market a long time are the ones where the buyer will often be more willing to come down significantly on the price.

The rule with making that initial offer is that you should always start low. The worst the seller can do is to turn down the offer. Likely they will make a counter-offer. If not, raise your offer a bit. The lower your offers, the lower the eventual counter-offer you are likely to get. Be patient and don't be rushed into a bad decision.

Don't bother getting a home inspection. It's just extra money spent and many of these clowns don't know what they are doing anyway. But DO inspect the house and property thoroughly yourself. If you have a brother-in-law who's a carpenter bring him along. Otherwise learn the ropes yourself as I did.

Start at the bottom of the house and work your way up. Check the foundation thoroughly for cracks, imperfections and moisture. If there is a crawl space make sure it is dry, then inspect the footings, sewer and water lines and where the electric and phone lines comes into the house. On the outside of the foundation, where it meets the siding, check for termites.

Next check the sewer, water and electric systems from inside the house by simply flushing the toilet, turning on water faucets and all lights and appliances. Inspect the breaker box to make sure all wires run inside walls from it and that there's nothing else funky about it.

Look for any cracks in the sheet rock and for windows that open poorly as these may indicate shifts in the foundation. Move up to the ceiling and look for any cracks or water stains that indicate leaks in the roof.

Check the attic and crawlspace for insulation and inspect the roof trusses. Then go outside and inspect fascia and roof for problems. Make sure all outside water spigots have good pressure. Inspect the well and sewage system.

Make sure there are no easement issues, liens or other problems with the place. When you close on the property you should always get either title insurance or an abstract. When you have *paid off* the property make sure to get a warranty deed and make sure a copy gets filed at the county courthouse.

That's about it.

After two and a half years at Alton, we put the place up for sale. After a year of listing with a realtor, we posted it ourselves on Craigslist. Within a month we sold it for $65,000.

Since the banks weren't lending at that time in 2009, we financed the sale. At first I was hesitant, but the buyer's put $10,000 down, agreed to keep it insured and have not missed a payment on their 15-year mortgage. The best part is that it provides us with a steady income of nearly $500/month.

When you buy a place, go through a realtor. The reality is that you simply gain access to many more listings than the much fewer and far between listings you'll find for sale by owner. Keep your eyes open for these too, of course, but realtors can all access the MLS database for their area and can show you everything for sale in the area by ALL realtors.

How you sell a place really depends on your location and situation. I've had good luck both ways. If you live in the boonies you may try a realtor as they can bring people to you from urban centers. If, on the other hand you are trying to sell that first or second shotgun shack or trailer in town, you may try to sell it yourself so that the little bit of profit you make doesn't all go to the realtor's commission. These commissions are often negotiable.

Insurance is one of the biggest scams known to man. Whenever we've owner-occupied a place we've never once bought property insurance. I didn't buy car insurance until they required you have it to register a car. Over those 15 years I ran outlaw, I saved thousands of dollars. We don't have health insurance either.

Screw big pharma, the hospital cartel, greedy doctors and the insurance mafia protection racket. These vampires should be avoided whenever possible, if not shot before firing squad.

When we have serious dental or medical needs we go to dentists in Argentina or doctors in Thailand or a pharmacy in Katmandu – where you can buy any medicine available for a hundred times cheaper than the US price due to the price controls on drug companies which nearly every other nation in the world imposes. You can also buy the medicine over the counter and without some high-priced *Illuminati* doctor writing you his condescending, insulting and many times dead wrong prescription.

Yes, you take a chance not having insurance, but you have to take some calculated prudent risks in this world to get ahead or you never will. The whole concept of insurance is a fear-based protection racket founded by the Knights Templar. The first insurance company in America was the Freemason-affiliated Modern Woodmen of America. What more do you need to know?

In the case of property insurance the key is to buy a cheap house in town or better yet a large piece of property in the country with a small house on it. This way if something happens to the house, which wasn't worth a mint because it was small, you still own the property and other improvements such as well, septic, etc.

This all fits well with the key to making money on housing, which is to start by buying something at the low end of the market that you can pay off in a few years or less. If this requires moving out of a high housing-cost area to the boondocks of Western North Dakota or northern Mississippi or here in the Ozarks, just do it.

By now you should have paid off all your credit card debt and been working overtime to save that grubstake of money for a down payment. Search the country by internet for low-priced housing options, quit your meaningless job and hit the road Jack!

Chapter 4

# Transportation

America has the worst public transportation system in the world. As such, we have become a car culture to the extreme. When you are ready to make that run for rural America, you will need a car.

In the meantime, if you are living in a city with decent public transportation or with good bike lanes, consider selling your car. You'll save lots of money on gas, insurance and maintenance. You can use the proceeds from the car to pay off your credit card debts and bolster your savings account grubstake.

Because you'll be walking and biking more, you can cancel that gym membership, because your whole life will become predicated on good exercise. Your mind will learn to slow down with the more natural pace of walking, liberating your brain from another of the matrix programmers' tools, which is to constantly speed us up.

You'll also see things that you never would have seen out of a car window. We spent the last two summers – one in Missoula, MT and one in Spearfish, SD – without a car. It was awesome.

Our friends Gene and Jo, who live in Missoula, are in their late 70's and they still refuse to buy a car. They bike everywhere and take the bus in winter if the weather is bad.

When you go too fast, you make bad decisions. Often you spend money on some needless item when, if you had the time, you could have achieved your aim another way. This feeds matrix corporations and erodes your grubstake.

If you live in or near a town, but your abode is a long way from work, a 49 CC scooter can also be a good choice. These things can be bought for around $500 brand new. You don't need insurance and you don't even need to register the thing in most states. And they get up to 100 MPG.

If you need to travel cross country, check the auto driveaway option I mentioned earlier. Universities often have "ride boards" where you can catch a lift or offer a ride to a certain destination. Craigslist also has a section for this. Gas is customarily split, making the ride cheaper for everyone.

If you can't score a lift in any of these ways, the notorious Greyhound is your next best car-less option. Make sure to buy your ticket 14 days in advance to get the best deal. It's literally cheaper than driving.

Yes, you'll run into some crazy-ass people, but as the economy has headed south and gas prices have soared, more "ordinary" folks are taking the bus as well.

About ten years ago, the Greyhound monopoly cut many smaller towns from its routes. As a result, access is more limited, buses are more crammed and the overall experience has become, well, rather hellish. But it's cheap, funny and you'll meet some good folks along the way, maybe even develop empathy for their collectively impoverished condition.

If you need to fly, you'll need to plan ahead. Courier flights used to be a great cheap way to travel, but post-911 they are virtually non-existent. Still, if you do your planning, your next flight can be FREE.

The best plan nowadays is to visit the various frequent flier sections of the major airline websites. Due to matrix merger mania, there are now only three in the domestic market – Delta Sky Miles, United Mileage Plus and American Advantage.

Go to the "Earn Miles" section under each of these frequent flier sections and see what's on offer. Ordinarily, you will be offered 25,000 to 40,000 miles just for signing up for a credit card connected to the various programs.

Most times you get the miles by simply using the card once. Buy a candy bar, wait for the miles to show up in your frequent flier account and then call in to cancel the card. Tell them you have too many credit cards, which you do if you have more than that one Visa card I talked about earlier.

The miles will show up in your frequent flier account within six weeks. With good planning, 25,000 miles gets you a free roundtrip ticket anywhere in the US. Book the seats at their website to avoid paying a fee reserving by phone. Also, check the advance requirements. Some airlines, like United, will charge you $80 each way if you book less than 21 days in advance.

One winter I got bored and systematically went after all the miles I could accumulate. The next winter my wife and I flew roundtrip from St. Louis to Buenos Aires, Argentina. We did a three-country loop of Argentina, Chile and Uruguay.

We drank good wine, ate top-notch tenderloin, viewed penguins in the South Pacific and visited the awesome Iguazu Falls. Our flights were had for 50,000 miles each, which I had racked up doing the matrix credit card shuffle. They were FREE!

Make a habit of constantly acquiring these miles and you'll fly free for the rest of your life. I just got 30,000 more miles last week by applying for the exact same card I had gotten another 30,000 miles for and canceled three months ago.

The thing you must remember about the matrix is that for all its blow about invincibility, it is actually extremely dumb, very slow and easily subdued.

You can also get newspaper and magazine subscriptions, Omaha Steaks, fine chocolates and a bunch of other cool stuff using airline miles. Many times in my life I've had the *Wall Street Journal* delivered to my door for free. Since this is one of the primary *Illuminati* mouthpieces in the world, reading it is a great way to track and document their crimes.

The key to the credit card shuffle is to stay on top of it. Use the card once, pay off the balance and cancel it immediately so you don't forget to do it later. The cards on offer all have annual fees starting in the second year. The first year is waived, but the banksters are counting on you to forget to cancel the card so they can stick you with the annual fee in perpetuity. If the first-year fee is not waived, don't apply for the card.

Using public transportation is great – it's a good thing to do and it's economical. But America is a car culture and eventually you're going to buy a car. Next to housing, this is the most important economic decision you'll have to make in your life. And you'll have to do it many times over, so you might as well make the extra effort to get good at it.

I use the same rules when buying cars as I do in procuring a house. Pay cash and look for a below-book-value deal that you can drive awhile and still make out on when you sell it later.

Most people automatically take out a loan to buy a car. This is a huge mistake. Interest payments, no matter how small, make you a debtor. You now must scramble to make this additional payment every month.

Equally usurious, is the full coverage insurance you'll be required to have any time you finance a vehicle. If you buy your car for cash, you have the option of purchasing only the bare minimum liability car insurance required by state law. I pay about $120 every six months for car insurance. If I had full coverage, I'd pay closer to $350 every six months.

GEICO has the cheapest car insurance.

This leads to another reason why you should NEVER buy a brand new car. With prices on new cars surging, buying a new car becomes even more of a trap. Even if you pay cash for it, you would feel the need to get full coverage insurance since you feel like you paid LOTS of cash for it and want to protect your "investment".

But if you buy a used car with a much lower book value, you will be more comfortable just getting liability insurance.

This leads me to the next reason never to buy a new car. It's a very bad "investment". The moment you drive it off the lot, the value will go down $5,000 or more.

When my wife moved in with me more than twenty years ago, she was driving a Mazda 626 that she bought brand new. We were broke and headed for Japan and she still had large car and full coverage insurance notes to pay on it.

When I first suggested that she sell it, she said, "Yeah but that's a new car".

I said, "Honey, sorry to break the news, but that is now most definitely a used car".

She sold it and made more than enough to pay off what she owed. We were down to my 63' Rambler station wagon, which I had traded for a .22 rifle and fixed the clutch on. I had earlier paid off her credit cards on the condition that she cut all up but one and with the extra money left over from selling her car, we became debt free.

We were bound for Japan so we drove the Rambler back to South Dakota where we visited my mom. The starter was going and Jill didn't know how to pop the clutch on the 3-speed to get it going on the fly.

All the way across Montana, I parked at the top of inclines whenever I shut the engine down. That way I could roll down hill, pop the clutch and start the engine.

But there are no hills to park on in the flatlands that is Faulkton, SD. I'll never forget the looks of mom's neighbors peeping out their curtained windows to watch my beautiful bride-to-be pushing that wagon down the street so I could pop the clutch and start it.

We sold the Rambler for $500 to a collector from Minneapolis who came all the way to Faulkton to buy it. We hopped a Greyhound to Kansas City and flew off to Japan to get our grubstake.

Generally, you want to take one of two strategies when buying a car. If you're young, consider buying that proverbial $500 – $1000 beater car. I've done this many times and if you inspect it well and take your time buying, you can get a dependable rig for a good price.

As I've gotten older and cars have gotten more difficult (by design) to work on, I've gone to buying late model cars only a few years old. Here, look for a gem car model hidden within an auto industry laggard.

The car I'm driving now is a 2007 Suzuki SX4. It's the only subcompact all-wheel drive available in the US. It's got a big hatchback, so I can haul large items. The private road we live at the end of is steep and rough, so it's great to have the 4-wheel-drive option. And I've gotten 39 MPG on the highway with it.

Suzuki is not known for making great cars, but unlike the rest of the Suzuki line – which is made in Korea – the SX4 is made entirely in Japan where it is the most popular car to drive, outselling all Toyota and Honda models there.

I checked for online reviews of the car. All gave it good marks and were pleasantly surprised by this diamond in the rough. I checked the KBB book value – as you should always do when buying or selling a car – and found that the car booked at over $10,000. With a few barely noticeable hail dings, his asking price was $6,995.

Because of the hail dings and the Suzuki name, we got it for $6,500. We've driven it almost a year now and love it. The KBB book on it is still $9,300, so any time I want to sell it I can actually make a profit.

NEVER BUY FROM A CAR DEALER!

This bunch is one of the lowest invertebrates- along with insurance salesmen – taking up space on this planet. Pathological liar seems to be a prerequisite for these callings.

Car dealers buy cars from individuals and auctions. They simply detail the car, mark it up astronomically, and sell it to you. Worse yet, they give you a pittance for your trade-in, which you should also never do. Sell your car outright and buy another one the same way.

If you think that buying a used car from a dealer is "safer", you're wrong. Unless you're given a written warranty, these shysters will no more fix your blown engine than would a private seller.

Do what a dealer does. Check your area for wholesale car auctions. We bought a Toyota minivan in Los Angeles this way after we returned from Japan.

Look into "salvage title" cars. In 2006, I bought a 2005 Ford Focus with 21,000 miles on it. It booked at over $10,000. I got it for $5,850 cash – a figure just low enough that I didn't have to worry about purchasing full coverage insurance.

The car came out of Memphis and probably belonged to a drug dealer. An adversary had attempted to stick a rag into the gas tank and start it on fire. The fire went out, so only the rear quarter panel and some sensors needed replacing. Still, the insurance company was forced to total it. Enter the salvage title dealer, who got it for a song, easily fixed it, made a buck and passed his savings along to me.

When buying these salvage title cars you must make sure that the damage done to the car isn't serious. The main thing is to make sure it doesn't have engine, transmission or frame damage. If it does, you'll know when you drive it. Also, look for uneven tire wear, though this doesn't always work since the dealer can change out tires easily.

If in doubt, get a CARFAX. If not in doubt, don't waste your money. I've never bought one.

I look at a car just like I look at everything else. When I buy one, the goal is to be able to drive it awhile and resell it for almost as much or more than I paid.

This premise is radically different from what most people do, which is to throw tens of thousands of dollars down the "shiny new financed car" hole through a lifetime.

In this world you must try to sell as much as you buy. In these modern urbanized times this will never be fully achieved, but to the extent you can close the gap, you will be increasingly liberated from the matrix.

Three other points about cars:

(1 It is far cheaper to own just one car at a time if you can help it. My wife and I share a car and we live in the middle of nowhere. Of course this may not be possible until you've shit-canned your "jobs".

(2 You should buy a car that gets a minimum of 30 miles per gallon. Don't buy into the "safety" argument about small cars. Don't buy a pickup or SUV unless you own a 50,000 acre cattle ranch in Wyoming, in which case you may actually need one. With regards to all other prospective "urban cowboys", I can often be heard muttering contemptuously, "Big truck, little dick", as they pass. Grow up!

(3 Avoid fairly old cars that still cost lots of money. That means avoid anything 2000-2005 that costs any more than a couple thousand dollars. These newer, but not new, cars aren't built as good as older ones and are a beast to work on.

Some good cars to look at in the beater class include the mid 80's to mid 90's Geo Metro, Subaru Justy, Ford Fiesta, Volkswagen Rabbit diesel and Plymouth Horizon. Pay no more than $1000 and closer to $500.

I once owned a 1988 Chevy Sprint – the precursor to the Metro. It was a 3-cylinder and got 55 MPG. They don't even make 3-cylinder cars anymore. Curious isn't it?

Otherwise buy a car that is no more than five years old and has no more then 60,000 miles on it. Craigslist can be a good place to find one of these. Local estate auctions can sometimes be even better than the wholesale auctions, since many people are there to buy other stuff and not to buy that one late model car on the block.

Good driving habits equal higher gas mileage. Starts and stops should be gradual, not sudden. A lower gear should be used when in hilly terrain. Inflate your tires near the maximum level.

Most people believe the myth that you should under-inflate your tires to be "safe". Actually this increases you chances of a blowout and vastly decreases your gas mileage. But at least the *Illuminati* oil barons will be happy.

Most car tires today say "Max 44 PSI". I run mine at around 40. Do you really think the matrix tire corporations would risk being sued if 44 PSI was one bit dangerous?

Chapter 5

# Food, Clothing & Bills

The system is constantly conjuring up ways to nickel and dime you. Americans have become incredibly naïve, far too trusting of a system which proves over and over on a daily basis that it most definitely cannot be trusted.

Conversely we have become far too cynical of the people, who do heroic things every day. We must reverse this dichotomy. Trust the people, do NOT trust the matrix.

Be generous to friends, family, the people and the natural world, but learn to be stingy in your dealings with the system. This is another one of those dogmas which must be examined.

The programmers are constantly sending out their message that frugality is a bad thing. That's not because they want you to buy your friend the next beer. You should. It's because they want you to recklessly open your purse strings and donate all your hard earned grubstake to the matrix shopping complex.

So, take it a step further. The best defense is a good offense in any sport. Rather than being led around by the nose by the matrix ad department, be audacious and proactive. While you make it a practice to spend as little of your freedom on their stuff, take advantage of opportunities you come across to nickel and dime the hell out of the matrix. It changes the whole power equation. Your grubstake savings will grow. And it's fun!

Little things add up when it comes to getting the grubstake necessary to bolt the matrix. Most people have some kind of space they can use to grow a garden. So get planting.

Don't go out and buy some fancy tiller. It won't break up new ground well anyway and will set you back hundreds of dollars. Buy a cheap shovel and start digging. Get to a depth of the length of the shovel blade, shake the dirt from the grass and weeds, and either discard the latter so it can't replant itself in your garden, or better yet, plant the clumps as sod in an eroded area that needs it.

It's a bit tedious, but efficient over time. Make sure you leave the heavy clay subsoil on the bottom. It other words don't turn it over, just get under it, pry it loose and chop it up leaving the topsoil on top where this better soil will feed the roots of your veggies.

Other than a shovel, your only expense should be garden seed. Don't buy high dollar seed from either corporate or boutique seed dealers. Buy the 5 for $1 seed packets at the Dollar Store or your local hardware store. After your first harvest, you can gather seed, which you can then use to plant your garden next year. This fresher seed germinates better and you can select the biggest seed and grow better vegetables. Soon you will spend NOTHING planting your garden.

As with all American pastimes, gardening has become a huge marketing opportunity for the matrix. Don't fall into that trap and buy a bunch of needless garden tools, fertilizer or topsoil. You don't need it. Stay out of Lowe's and Home Depot. They are high-dollar money pits full of nothing you need.

It's amazing what kind of soil seed will grow in. Brainwashed modern capitalist man vastly underestimates the wealth of historical knowledge within a seed, because we are alienated so badly from nature, including our own nature.

So we decide the matrix knows better than the soil and buy topsoil at Lowe's that could have easily come from a polluted job site, or bring in $100 truck loads of "good topsoil" that is usually full of invasive weeds, moles and herbicides. Save your money. Use the soil you have. Have faith in nature.

Go organic for the same reasons, and because going organic costs less and works better. All that high dollar weed killer and chemical fertilizer will do is deplete your savings, give your family cancer and scare away all the good bugs, frogs, lizards and snakes which, left to their own devices, will handily eat the "bad" bugs in your garden if given a chance.

The easiest way to compost is to collect all coffee grounds, food waste and scraps to use as compost. We set one of those 34 oz. plastic Folgers coffee containers by the kitchen sink. Everything except meat scraps – which will attract unwanted nighttime critter visitors – goes in the bucket.

The more compost and organic matter you add to your soil, the better the tilth of your soil, the more good bugs are attracted to your garden, the less bad bugs can reside there. It is both simple and quite amazing, as many simple things tend to be.

Don't go to the work of a compost pile. Sheet composting is just as effective. When your kitchen compost container gets full, simply spread it around plants in the garden. Hit a different area each time. Let nature do the rest.

Once your plants have come up, mulching your garden will supplant the need for much weeding and keep your topsoil moist through dry periods, which allows you to water much less. If you pay for your water, this also saves you money.

We use oak leaves, because we live in an oak forest and have them in abundance, but use whatever you can find readily and nearby in your ecosystem for mulch. If you have a mulching mower, grass clippings are excellent high-nitrogen mulch. If you don't have a mulching mower, you can still rake the clippings onto your garden. Wood chips, sawdust and straw are other good mulches. Sometimes you can get wood chip mulch delivered for free from the utility company as they clear the power lines in your area. Never buy mulch.

At harvest time, most vegetables can be frozen or canned. We freeze everything except tomatoes, which we can. Instead of canning our cucumbers, we make refrigerator pickles in a large glass candy jar. Just make up your spice mix – using dill, garlic, onion and whatever else from your garden blended into vinegar and water – and put the mix in that glass jar in the refrigerator. Add cucumbers as they ripen and within days you have fresh pickles without all the fuss of canning.

Still, learn to can as well, because once you get a self-sufficient garden going, you won't be able to fit all your tomatoes in the freezer. And the only way to make a large batch of salsa is to can it. Don't forget to grow some essential cilantro for that.

Speaking of herbs, why not grow your own oregano, thyme, mint, lemon balm, fennel, sage, rosemary and tarragon. These are all perennials, so once you plant them, they come back every year on their own. Egyptian walking onions are a great perennial onion to grow as well.

Each May we cut and dry our own stash of kitchen herbs. My wife has written a book about it (see Jill's blog, Show Me Oz at www.ShowMeOz.wordpress.com). After years of trying different methods, we've found the best way to dry the most flavorful herbs is also the simplest. Go figure.

You simply cut the herbs and remove the leaves from stems. Toss the stems back on your garden as mulch/compost. Spread the leaves out on whatever stainless steel baking pans you have. Set the pans on a hot sidewalk or in any area with full sun.

The pan's reflective heat dries the herbs fast. Drying herbs fast – but not too fast or too hot as in an oven – preserves maximum flavor.

The old Ozark method is to put those same reflective baking pans on the dash board of your car. If I want to dry something really fast I use this method. It works very well, but keep a close eye on your herbs. If you leave them on that dashboard a bit too long, they can get a little crispy.

We just dried a quart jar (three baking pans dried down and crushed) of Egyptian onion greens today.

Don't waste your money on one of those nifty-sounding food dehydrators. I did once. These contraptions take far too long to dry anything. As a result, you lose lots of flavor. Using one also adds to your electric bill.

Spices at the grocery store have been sitting on a truck for God knows how long. The expensive micro-bottles are flavorless. Grow your own spices. You won't believe the difference in flavor, nutrition and quantity. You'll soon have big jars full of the stuff.

Perennials are the key to a self-sufficient garden. Other great perennials to grow include strawberries, raspberries, asparagus, horseradish, sorrel, rhubarb and Jerusalem artichokes.

If you live where you can raise animals, go for it. I just finished our chicken coop and goat/pig pen last week. I used salvaged lumber, fence posts, roofing tin and wire that we came across cleaning up the property. I bent crooked nails. I got some hinges from a friend who works at a big factory, then improvised on some latches for the gates. We scored some paint near a dumpster on the way home one day so I could paint the gates – bright orange. In the end, I didn't spend one penny on the construction of this critter pen.

Animals can provide meat, milk, eggs, leather and warm winter clothing. Their manure is essential to keeping your garden healthy.

Hunting, fishing and gathering are also important ways to dodge the matrix and its expensive processed toxic GMO food.

I've been filling our freezer with wild black raspberries and blackberries of late. We put away 13 gallons this year. We gather black walnuts and persimmons in the fall.

If we pass a house where a fruit tree is going unpicked, we stop to inquire if they'd mind if we pick some. Offer to leave some with the owner in exchange for the favor, especially if the owner is elderly. Other times, we've found fruit trees at public fishing accesses and the like, and harvested this fruit.

Find out what wild edibles grow in your area and start looking around for foraging opportunities. There is nothing like the feeling of picking fruit or nuts that nature has provided for free. And you didn't even have to plant them. Jah really does provide. You just have to pay attention and be audacious.

Still, no matter how self-sufficient we become, most all of us will have to buy some food at a matrix supermarket. Food is central to life and shopping for food can make or break your plans to exit the matrix. Shopping for food is an art. And it is a war.

Where you shop is important. Never buy food from a convenience store, gas station or one of those high-priced snobby organic food places like Whole Foods Market. What a scam!

If you have a farmer's market in your area, these are great places to buy local produce. Look for farmers in your area willing to sell you a half a beef or hog. Look for signs on the road nearby for people selling eggs and other produce.

We are fortunate in this area to have many salvage grocery stores. These grocers buy large lots of food that didn't sell at regular supermarkets. Often it's a new flavor of a product that didn't take off. Other times the items are near or just past the expiration date.

Most of these stores are well kept and clean, though occasionally we've come across one that looks more like a botulism laboratory. Those are weeded out quickly and soon close their doors.

We focus on two stores within 45 miles of our home. Once every two months we go to one or the other and spend maybe $125. At that distance you need to stock up to make the trip worthwhile and so that you have to go less often.

Look for no-frills groceries in your area. These are the ones that do not provide free shopping bags and where you shop shelves full of items still in the shipping boxes. Grab an empty box and use that to carry your groceries. The prices are lower than at conventional stores. The German chain, Aldi, is an excellent choice in our area.

Then there are the supermarkets. Make sure to visit each of these behemoths in your area to find out which one consistently offers the best prices on food. If you really compare, you will find that Walmart is never it, despite their propaganda to the contrary. Remember, their slogan is not "Always the Lowest Price", it's "Always *Low* Prices". Walmart sucks!

If you have several supermarkets nearby, shop their weekly sales. Get in the habit of stocking up on the very best deals each store has that week. You can research their sale ads on the internet or by simply browsing the ads when you walk in the door.

Shop slowly and only buy those very best deals, then go to the next store and do the same. Eventually your home will be filled with most of the necessary ingredients for any meal.

Stocking up is very often not a good strategy. I have even noticed in recent years, as people have taken to this practice, that you can often buy a smaller container of a certain product for less per ounce than you'd pay for the "economy" size. I guess that's code for helping the matrix economy out, because it sure doesn't help your economy.

The worst way to shop is to decide on what you want to cook for just one night and then go off to the store looking for the specific ingredients required. Since most of it will not be on sale, you will pay an arm and a leg. This one small tweak in the way you shop can be huge.

Use coupons when you can find them. You can sometimes combine in-store coupons with manufacturers' coupons and get items virtually free.

Only shop the outside aisles of grocery stores. Generally you'll find the sale items at either end of store aisles. The healthier fresh meat, dairy and produce will be on the outside of the store. The inside aisles are full of high-dollar, over-processed junk food.

If you start to eat nutritious food, you won't be as hungry and will in turn succumb less to expensive processed junk food snacks.

Another important thing to start doing is to add up the cost of your groceries as you shop. By doing this, you will soon become more familiar with what a "good price" is on various foods. You will also not get nickel-and-dimed by the matrix supermarket's rigged cash registers.

Check your receipt carefully after checkout and compare the total with what you added up as you shopped. I can't tell you how many times we've had to correct a cashier or go to customer service for a refund on an overcharge.

Most people are totally oblivious to this systematic slow bleed of their wallet. It seems to occur more at stores that use the in-house discount cards, which can easily confuse a customer at the register since items ring up full price and the card discount is deducted at the end. Keep an especially close eye on this if you shop at Safeway.

Eating out is where many people squander their grubstake. Many wage slaves feel that because they put in all those long hours for the man, they deserve to splurge often at over-priced restaurants. If you like eating usually bland, many times contaminated food, tipping an often rude waitress, and watching your savings whither, then go for it.

On the subject of tipping; I used to be a prep cook, and trust me, the hardest workers in a restaurant don't get squat from your tips. Plus, it allows the owner to underpay his employees, with you picking up the tab through your tip.

Of course, on the rare occasion that you do eat out, you should still leave a tip. Until we can reconfigure this broken part of the system, servers have to rely on tips to earn their full wages. Conversely, this injustice is also as good a reason as any not to eat out much.

That being said, there's nothing wrong with treating yourself once in awhile. My wife and I probably eat out every two weeks or so. When you do so, use a coupon or look for advertised specials. With the internet, they're everywhere. Eat at a family-owned restaurant to support your local economy and choose something you really like that is difficult to cook at home.

I have to tell you, though, that once you grow a garden or raise some chickens, most restaurant food will no longer even be appealing to you. Last night I picked a beet, carrot and green bean medley for dinner. You can't even *get* that at a restaurant. Nor could you get the custard pie with blackberry sauce that Jill kindly made us for dessert.

Clothing should take up virtually NONE of your hard-earned cash. We buy only shoes, socks and underwear. Most everything else we have gotten visiting friends and family, who were "just going to take numerous bags of clothes they were tired of to Goodwill".

Once you get the "simple liver" rap, people who know you EXPECT to dump their out-of-fashion clothes on you. Wear it as a badge of honor. Be the coyote. Live off of what the system throws away.

Dumpster-diving can also be quite lucrative in the area of clothing, though we've procured perfectly good refrigerators, computers, couches and beds this way, as well.

There are simply too many clothes in the world. One trip to Africa will convince you of that. There, ships full of used US, Japanese and European clothing arrive to be resold at village markets. Don't buy clothes, let them come to you. And they will.

Stay away from name-brand products. My friend, Jim, used to work at a household battery factory in NW Missouri. He says they shipped the exact same batteries out of the place, labeling some Duracell and other high-dollar brands, and others with cheap generic brands. The batteries were exactly the same except for the labels.

Monthly household bills can consume a huge percentage of a paycheck, which could have otherwise gone into that grubstake savings account. If you're struggling to save and/or need to get out of debt, start by cutting off your cable/satellite TV and your internet service. I didn't have either until I was in my late 30's and saved thousands of dollars as a result. I didn't even have a phone for a number of years.

TV is the central component in matrix programming plans to ensure your slavery. Whether you are aware of it or not, TV commercials and "programs" are constantly telling you how to be obedient and "fit in" through shopping and by being a sheeple. Getting rid of your television is quite a liberating experience.

The internet can also be a monumental waste of time. If you need it, you can access it at every public library in the land and many colleges and university libraries, as well. One of the worst decisions you can make is to have a mobile device with a high monthly charge that allows you to text or Facebook away your precious time and money!

If you do have cable/satellite or internet service at home, check your bills carefully. These companies are notorious in the nickel-and-dime arena. Never buy their "equipment protection plans". I recently had trouble with both my phone and my TV. In both cases, I was able to sign up for these repair plans the same day I needed things fixed.

Pay for the service one month or as required, get you stuff fixed for free, then drop the service. And don't forget to get your "time without service" credit, which will likely more than pay for that one-month of the extra charge.

Choose either a cell phone or land line, but not both. Such duplication is a waste of money. If you have kids, don't spoil them by buying them each a cell phone and an internet computer and a TV for their room. Just because the other wage slaves in the neighborhood choose to unwittingly destroy their children's minds by hard wiring them to the matrix, doesn't mean you have to.

Be a parent, teach your kids why this junk is detrimental and they will respect you more for it in the end. You'll also save lots of grubstake money.

Try to starve the power company monkey as much as possible. In winter, try keeping your thermostat at around 64 degrees in the day and turned down to 59 degrees at night. Wear a sweater by day and put an extra blanket on the bed at night.

In summer, open your windows overnight as much as possible. We only resort to air conditioning at night when the overnight lows hit around 75 degrees. Otherwise it's much less stuffy, more comfortable, healthier and, yes, cheaper to open those windows.

If you've escaped the matrix day job routine and are at home, leave the windows open in the morning until it gets hot outside. Shut windows and sunny side blinds during the heat of day and open them again when it has cooled down. If it gets stuffy in the afternoon, run the A/C for a few hours, then turn it off and open the windows an hour or so later. Try running you're A/C at 77 degrees and use "energy saver" mode, if available.

If you have access to free firewood, consider getting a woodstove. We love ours. I don't even have a chainsaw. It's just an extra expense, fossil fuel driven, dangerous, and not necessarily easier.

I use a $4 bow saw and cut smaller downed (and already seasoned) timber no bigger than four inches in diameter. It's easy to cut (the bow saw was a great invention since its small thin blade offers less resistance and cuts through wood like butter), there is no splitting required and the smaller wood burns hotter so less is needed. Best of all I've not paid the oil cartel one dime.

Unplug all you can when you go to bed at night and when not using an appliance. Put up a clothes line to dry your laundry. Once we got ours put up at the new place, I unplugged the electric dryer and haven't used it since. Just by pulling that greedy 220 plug, we now save $5-$7 off our monthly electric bill. Last month it was $45 and most of that was the $25 minimum charge.

If you live in a rural area, there is no reason to get trash service. Simply dig yourself a shallow fire pit well away from any structures or trees. Organize your trash into compost, burnables and what we call "outbound" trash – mainly metal and glass.

I burn anything that will burn. Some of my "environmentally-conscious" friends cringe at the idea of burning plastics, but I feel it is far more irresponsible to have someone else ship your trash off to a giant toxic landfill in some poor neighborhood and force those residents to suffer the health consequences.

Better to have to personally endure a small plume of noxious smoke once in awhile to remind you to consume less.

If you sort your trash this way, you will be blown away at how little "outbound" trash you generate. Never buy "garbage bags". Simply recycle grocery store bags. Use these as your trash bags.

When we go to town once a week, we take our one grocery store bag of outbound trash and deposit it at a gas station or mega-store trash receptacle. The trash man will survive without your monthly check.

This is another good reason to stay out of the inside aisles at the matrix supermarket, since this is where the nutrition-less, landfill-consuming canned items lurk. You can't burn a can.

If you have recycling facilities use them.

Never buy dish rags. Cut up old worn out clothes and bath towels for this task. Cut out all the various high-dollar specialty cleaning products, too. Vinegar, baking soda and dish soap will clean anything from your car to your toilet.

A particularly irksome development of late is this liquid bath soap craze. Isn't it obvious that a bar of soap lasts longer, is easier to use, doesn't get wasted and is way cheaper than this creepy liquid stuff that doesn't even seem to get you clean?

Never buy envelopes. You'll accumulate plenty in the mail from different places. Recycle them. Never buy paper. Recycled mail works fine. You can cut some sheets of these up to make smaller note pads.

Speaking of note pads, I'm a big believer in making lists each and every day of the things you need to do that day. This is especially true if you have wriggled out of that matrix job and are now relying on your own hard work and efficiency to stay free.

Lastly, keep track of your expenses every day. At the end of the month compare what you've spent with what you've earned.

Our income last month was only $1,288. But we spent only $533, adding $750 that month to our grubstake. Not bad for a couple of hillbillies.

Chapter 6

# Mercenary Shopping

Shopping for frivolous and unnecessary items consumes way too much of most people's time and budget, while chaining the new owner of this junk to a cluttered garage, a storage unit and general sedentary misery.

Still there are certain tools and entertainments we wish to procure and there are many good ways to get them other than at a store.

Again it is all about attitude. You must develop a resistance to shopping. It should be viewed as morally reprehensible. When you need to attain an item, do your research and find out where to get it at the best price, preferably – except, I would argue, in the case of electronics – used. Remember, the system has declared war on your family. Don't shop much. And fight like a mercenary of the revolutionary army when you must shop.

Barter is an ancient and excellent system which should be taken up across the land. Here, the palpable stench of their bloody fiat currency is absent.

When we lived on that 20 acre place near Peace Valley, we always had a bumper strawberry crop. Everyone likes strawberries, so we traded our excess for pasture-raised poultry, eggs and honey.

We also did a community-supported agriculture swap with a local dentist, whereby we exchanged a weekly run of in-season fresh vegetables from our garden for a good amount of dental work.

Most people have been trained to be timid when it comes to asking a "professional" to barter their service for your goods/services. In doing so, you are undervaluing your own efforts. It doesn't hurt to ask. Remember, be audacious.

This spring, my wife organized a seed swap where gardeners from all over the area came to trade seeds and plants. The 35-40 people in attendance all came away with lots of free garden seeds and plants, while passing on their extras to others! We met some great new people and got to hang out with some old friends. And the matrix was shut out.

On another recent occasion our good friends Phil and Amber got a bunch of trees from the Missouri Conservation Department. Phil then proceeded to dislocate his knee. Unable to plant all those trees and being the generous guy he is, he organized a tree giveaway. A handful of people showed up and each of us in turn brought various plants of our own to give way. Some of us brought food to share. Phil shared his excellent home-brewed dark brown ale. Everyone came away with something new to plant. No money was exchanged.

When we lived in Missoula, MT there was an event every May which came to be known as Hippy Christmas. This was the time when all those college students left their dorms and apartments to go home for summer break or move elsewhere. The alleys, parking lots and streets near the University of Montana would gradually fill up with all manner of goodies that these youngsters had left behind.

Since college has become very expensive, the kids that do attend universities nowadays are sadly from increasingly wealthy families. As a result, chances are good that their parents have bought them everything they could possibly need – and more – to fill their college abode, so what do these *trustafaris* care if some of these almost brand new pieces of furniture, appliances and gadgets go sitting curbside come summer break because it wouldn't fit in their shiny new Subaru Forester?

Dumpster diving is always above average in college towns because of this ongoing gentrification of our higher education system. But keep your eyes open in any town.

Another good opportunity for "ground scores" occurs when people move out of an apartment. They usually can't fit everything in their vehicle, so they tend to leave many excess items sitting beside the apartment complex dumpster. Look for the big piles.

I've known people who made a living off of this phenomenon, scooping up these unwanted items and selling them on Craigslist or at a yard sale.

We helped pioneer Missoula's anarchist market in the mid 1990's. Anyone could set up a table and sell whatever for free. It may have been the biggest of its kind in the country. It was too free for the white fathers on City Council and has since been corralled and added to the city balance sheet.

Our friend Erin used to dumpster dive stuff and bring it to the market to sell. How's that for audacious?

Speaking of Craigslist, if you need a specific item, it is often a good place to get it at less than half the store price. It is an even better place to *sell* unwanted items, since there is no commission like there is on EBay.

A good rule is, if you need to buy a more expensive item, go through your house and find something to sell to offset the purchase. You'll be surprised how easy it is to find such an item.

Auctions can be another great place to get things on the cheap. My wife and I had just moved into our new place here last fall and had previously been traveling ultra-light.

After we sold the Alton place, we ditched nearly everything. I bought us a series of one-way tickets that took us from Chicago-Dublin-Abu Dhabi-Johannesburg-Katmandu-Bangkok-Vancouver.

We fulfilled a lifelong dream of going on a safari in South Africa's Kruger National Park and during our five-country tour of southern Africa, also got to visit the majestic Victoria Falls on the Zimbabwe/Zambia border.

After another 8-month stint in Thailand, Laos and Malaysia, followed by consecutive summers in Missoula and Spearfish, we were ready to get back to the land.

We arrived at our new place with literally a couple of backpacks. I had never owned less in my life and it felt great. But now we needed to furnish our new home.

In October, we went to an auction nearby. I bid on five different lots of stuff. We jammed it into the car and still had to tie some things on top. We got numerous pieces of furniture, blankets,

Corning Ware, baking sheets and pans, dishes and all kinds of other stuff for a grand total of $8.

There are a couple of things to remember at auctions. You have to realize that the auctioneer is trying to maximize his/her commission by pushing up the prices on items. Though a friendly dance, you must realize that he is your adversary for this day.

Show up early so you can survey the entire premises and see what's for sale. If you see boxes of stuff you want you can nudge those different boxes together. If you do so, the auctioneer may very well sell those boxes as a single lot.

Once you've lined out your bid targets, move well away from those items so as not to draw the interest of other bidders or the auctioneers. Stay extra cool and disinterested because you don't want either other bidders or the auctioneer to think you really want those items.

Otherwise, there could be a bidding war or the auctioneer could activate a straw bidder, and the price goes up. Wait until well into the bid process on that item has commenced to cast your first bid. Let at least one other person bid first.

If a bunch of people start bidding, walk away. The item will sell too high. If it's just you and one other person, let time pass before your second bid. Slow the process down. Sometimes if you wait long enough to cast that first bid, no one else bids. Then the auctioneer will say, "Who wants it all for $1?"

You do! Score!

In this area we have several radio stations that do shows with names like *Tradio* and *Swapline*, where people call in to buy, sell and give away their items. This is another excellent way to sell and procure items outside the matrix store system.

Bulletin boards at libraries, universities and stores are also excellent places to sell big ticket items that won't fetch enough money at a yard sale. Make a list of items you wish to sell on a sheet of paper. Write "Must Sell!" at the top. Beside each item give a short description and your asking price. Write your phone number on the main sheet, then also write your number sideways on several little tear-offs at the bottom.

Bulletin boards can also be great places to find deals on stuff you need. Again, check university bulletin boards at the end of semesters when students have burned through their cash and want to lighten their moving load.

A major benefit of all of the above ways to acquire stuff is that you don't have to pay sales tax.

No store represents the evils of the matrix more than Wal-mart. As such, you should avoid shopping there. But it is an excellent place to "borrow" things.

How often do you need a certain tool or whatever for one project? You buy the thing, use it once and it sets it your garage taking up space and gathering dust for the next fifty years.

This is where the Chinese sweat shop, otherwise known as Wal-mart, comes in.

This particularly nefarious beast just happens to offer a 90-day return policy on most items. Make sure to keep your receipt. With it, you get cash back and won't need an ID. Without it, you'll get a Wal-mart store card for the amount and a bad mark on the matrix "naughty kids" list.

Get what you need, use it and return it with receipt for a cash refund. There is nothing illegal about it. It is Wal-Mart's policy and was their idea, not yours or mine.

You can abuse other Big Box stores in a similar manner. During that first meager Ozarks stint, I bought a mower at Walmart, used it for a full three months, returned it in totally hammered condition for cash; then bought one at Kmart and did the exact same thing three months later.

It is very important that you NEVER do this to a Mom & Pop store. This should go without saying, but it's amazing how many people don't get that distinction. Mom & Pop are not the owners of the matrix. In fact, they are clobbered by it daily, just as you are.

When you abuse these matrix corporate stores – who have gutted every Main Street in this country – you actually help the smaller stores by taking a bite out of Wal-Mart's bottom line. Equally important, you are also helping to set yourself free from the matrix.

The only better policy than mercenary shopping is no shopping. Chronic shopping will only take you further into the matrix prison. My wife and I go to town once a week. For us, it's not, "Buy Nothing Day", it's "Buy Nothing Week"– EVERY week.

It's not just that shopping keeps you in debt, penniless and anchored to the grid via a job. Material possessions also severely limit your mobility, increase your worries (since with each new item purchased you now have more to lose), and have a generally dampening effect on your potentially revolutionary spirit.

As Henry David Thoreau so eloquently put it, "Material possessions are a positive hindrance to the elevation of mankind".

Chapter 7

# Sell More than You Buy

We live in the belly of the beast, a declining empire, a super-sized narcissistic complacent nation – long dependent on the sweat, exploitation and resource largesse of the developing world.

Most Americans no longer produce anything. They only consume. And they have no clue what was required to get that cup of Starbucks Sumatran dark roast in their hand. They not only do not produce anything themselves, they are also entirely disconnected from the production process.

If we are going to turn this country around, and if you are going to exit the matrix, that has to change.

Start by become a producer of something. It doesn't matter what it is. It could be garlic or art or eggs or jewelry. It could be a service people need, such as home baking (which my sister Lisa wisely does around the Holidays), landscaping, a shuttle service, or whatever. Just find something that fits your circumstance, or better yet, something you enjoy.

There are farmer's markets, art shows and flea markets all over this country that will provide you a venue to sell whatever it is you produce.

Becoming a producer empowers you by providing an offset to those things you must buy. It gives you an edge *vis-à-vis* the system. And it also can give your life new meaning and purpose.

When most mainstream economists – both liberal and conservative – are asked what the US economy needs to get out of its funk, they will repeat the same refrain that, "the consumer needs to start spending more again". I would argue just the opposite.

The main problem with the US is that it has become a rather heavy-set, satisfied, lazy beast. Conspicuous consumption is rampant. Ingenuity and innovation are grinding to a halt. Many are flat afraid of ANY type of manual labor.

The economy has been decimated by a parasitic financial capitalism whose *modus operandi* is laziness. These are the touted "job creators", who in reality are the, "job destroyers". The matrix cheerleaders on CNBC call this bunch, the "financial services" industry.

These idle rich button-pushers specialize in wealth *destruction* through mergers, downsizing, speculation, derivatives, dark pools, "worker productivity", insurance settlements and the like.

What we do not need is more speculation and consumption.

What we do need is production.

First, we need to break up the monopolistic cartels that rule nearly every industry, stifling competition. To help create this new competition we then need far more Americans to become producers.

But to become a producer, you need time away from the 9-5 rat race. And to get away from that, you'll need to raise some cash.

Start by getting rid off all the needless shit that clutters your life, has put you in debt, has you pinned down in a cubicle and clouds your ability to even think clearly.

Yard sales are a highly underrated way to get rid of all the stuff clogging those plastic storage bins in your attic or garage. Most things in your house constitute unnecessary clutter. Selling them can pay down debt, put money in your pocket, even allow you to quit your job and start producing something.

Once a year commit to having a three or four day yard sale. We go Thursday-Sunday, leaving most of it out overnight unless it rains. The hardest part is getting all the stuff in and out the door, so you may as well do four days if you can, before bringing what's left – always much less – back in.

Don't bother with newspaper ads, unless they are free or super cheap. Instead, focus on good sign placement. Start with a sign at a major intersection or two near your place. Use a big arrow on those signs. Put the same colored arrows on the next ones until you hit your driveway. Three or four signs should do it.

Make them out of free cardboard and a black magic marker. Add some color as an eye-catcher if you can. Secure the signs firmly to something. I usually nail them part way into a power pole, then bend the nails down to firm them up and so that they and the nails will come out easily. Leave the signs up day and night during the sale, and make sure to remove them when you're finished.

If you're moving, start early and have one or two weekends of moving sales. We always start our moving sales *before* we've even sold a house. Your house will actually sell sooner with less clutter in it. People want to envision their own stuff in a house when they are looking to buy. Your stuff will just make the place look smaller.

Having the moving sale early sends the universe a signal of intention that we are ready to move on. This creates momentum towards selling the house. Be proactive.

Each time we've moved on we've made a few thousand extra dollars just by having that moving sale. By getting rid of stuff, you also save money renting a U-Haul or a storage unit. And traveling light between places allows you the mobility to embark upon that dream trip you've always wanted to take.

Stuff is just stuff. You can always get more. If you wish to bail the matrix, it is extremely important that you lose your attachment to your stuff.

Obviously there are sentimental items which you'll want to take with you and that's fine. We do the same. But all other things can be procured when you've settled in again, often in newer condition and many times at a lower price or even free if you keep those coyote eyes open.

Bigger ticket items do not sell that well at yard sales. You're better off using Craigslist or radio call-in shows, like *Tradio*, to buy appliances, nice furniture, electronics, instruments, equipment, etc. *Tradio* is an even better place to sell these types of things.

Start selling these items even before you launch your moving sale because it sometimes takes more time to sell the more expensive items.

Take whatever doesn't sell at your yard or moving sale to a nearby pawn shop. The owner will usually give you another $50-

$100 for the rest of it. If not drop it off at a local church or thrift store. They'll be glad to have it.

Many people I know seem to have that pesky few thousand dollars in credit card debt that they just can't seem to escape. With interest rates of 15 % or more, this is literally a giant Goldman Sachs vampire squid wrapped around your neck.

If these people would simply sell a few big ticket items and have a once-yearly yard sale, they could easily pay off those usurious credit cards and burn them.

But the best part of trading all this useless stuff for cash and paying down debt is that it's gone. I guarantee you will feel better.

It will be easier to remember where more useful possessions are at again, you'll be more organized and feel liberated from the clutter energy that had begun to permeate your abode, compliments of the matrix.

Nickels and dimes add up and making them add up is the key to matrix emancipation.

Along the way, don't get suckered into one of those get rich quick schemes. I should know. I tried many of them in my youth and I lost money every single time.

When I was in college a guy who lived a few rooms down in the dormitory told me soybeans futures were going to the moon. He got me to match his $1,500 and together we bought a March contract. At first the price went up. I said we should cash in. He said wait. The price then swooned, we got a margin call and our $3,000 was gone. I had to borrow money from my mom. Ugh!

Another time, I bought bonds from some traveling shyster operating out of the offices of my local bank for the day. He lied to me directly about the inverse relationship between a bond price and its yield. Or he was such a shill or idiot that he really didn't even know.

At any rate, I put $3,000 into a bond mutual fund and watched the yield go steadily up, which he had told me was what I wanted to happen. You actually want the yield to go lower which causes the *price* of the bond to go up. I took another haircut.

But I'd also learned a valuable lesson about investing in the rigged casino, otherwise known as Wall Street. I haven't sent a dime in that direction for 25 years. And I never again will.

If you have money in that heart of the matrix that is Wall Street, do whatever it takes and get it out. It's about to crash again. Don't be a fool!

I tried both Amway and Juice Plus multilevel marketing scams and again lost money. These are basically Ponzi schemes where the first few people who started the company make money every time some unknowing SOB – like me – buys cases of product and tries to resell them.

Most times the person is unable to sell this much ballyhooed high-priced junk. If he does sell product, those above him in the pyramid get a cut.

If, much more likely, he falls on his face, those insiders have still made money selling him/her the initial product. If these financial parasites can sell just one case of their snake oil to a million new recruits, they've sold a whole lot of product.

That's the secret to the scam that goes under the Orwellian name of "multilevel marketing". Stay away from ALL of it.

It really is true – unless you sell your soul and go to work as a trader for Goldman Sachs –there is no shortcut to getting ahead. Hard work pays off. So does living frugally. It's that simple.

Also remember that the turtle wins the race. Start slowly on your noble path towards matrix emancipation. Make lists. Go at your own pace, but be persistent. Keep at it. If you stumble, get back up again and keep moving forward. Put your boots on soldier.

Be a warrior in the fight to make your country great again, and yourself whole again.

This is War!

Chapter 8

# The Grubstake

The goal of all of the above is to first get out of debt and then to start saving money, for this is the grubstake you will need to get free from the urbanized prison you live in which is a wholly-owned cash cow for the matrix.

Remember that little things add up. And lots of little things can add up surprisingly fast. If at any point along the way while saving that grubstake, you still have debt, pay it off immediately. Then stay out of debt for the rest of your life.

At some point you will cease to give a shit about your all-important "credit rating" – one of the central *Illuminati* fear tools to keeping its slaves in line. This disgusting financial parasite branch of the matrix is lorded over by three spooky private companies cozy with the national security apparatus, who keep a healthy dossier on every American.

At some liberating point, your "credit rating" will not matter, because credit is a *bad* thing that makes you a debtor and you will want nothing more to do with it.

Another very important old adage (amazing how many of these anachronisms turn out to be true) to remember is that it's not how much money you *make*, it's how much money you *save* that counts.

There are many financial downsides to having a "job" that are not often considered. First, there's the expense of getting to and from your workplace, for which you are not compensated and which has become increasingly expensive as gas prices skyrocket.

You'll also have to buy clothing for that job, sometimes even – God forbid – an expensive monkey suit which mimics the ridiculous power-tripping matrix.

You'll also need to eat something mid-shift and for most matrix slaves, company food is no longer free. Nowadays carpenter hires are even told to "bring your own tools". It's ridiculous and degrading how working people are treated in this country.

Get in the habit of packing your own lunch from home; otherwise, you'll squander your precious grubstake at some overpriced chain restaurant or diabetes-laden fast-food joint.

Make your own coffee and breakfast too, so you don't end up veering into some cartel-owned gas station for a high-priced muffin.

There are also payroll deductions for income tax, Social Security and Medicare. These take a huge bite out of your paycheck and reduce your hourly pay quite dramatically.

My wife and I strive to remain just below the threshold for which a couple is required to pay federal income tax. We are legal war resisters. The threshold this year was around $19,000. We made a little over $18,000. Perfect!

Since we don't have paychecks, we don't have deductions. I've worked "real jobs" so sporadically over the years that any time I did get a "real job" I would always request a W-4 form from my new employer.

This little known IRS form asks two questions: (1 did you make enough money last year to owe federal taxes? (2 do you expect to make enough money this year to owe federal taxes?

If you can answer "yes" to both questions (more importantly the first, since the second is hypothetical and anyone can and should answer "yes" to it), you can sign this form, have your employer sign and they will submit it to the IRS. Once this is done you will not have federal income tax withheld from your paycheck.

A big reason why owner-occupied housing is such a great investment is that after you've lived there for two years you can sell it without owing any capital gains tax.

If you use this strategy – as we have for years – you can maintain an income just below the federal tax threshold, but still bring in those BIG chunks of nontaxable income each time you sell that house you've lived in rent-free for two years or more.

Yes, this strategy is predicated on moving, but I can tell you that we've enjoyed our opportunities to see the country and the world by living in different places, and also by traveling somewhere nice in between owning each place.

I can also tell you that the place we live now, which we paid cash for less than a year ago, is the coolest place we've ever lived. So despite certain inconveniences, we're both really glad we kept moving until we found this place.

We're also glad we were patient, working our way up to this totally private 42 acres at the end of the road with a new cabin and some good outbuildings and fences.

Too many people go for that dream home too early in life. As a result they take on a massive mortgage payment which – in a down housing market like we are experiencing now in which selling a house is difficult – becomes a giant albatross around their necks.

Start with a fixer upper or three and work your way up to that dream place. Borrow on the first, pay it off, sell it, and pay cash from then on. Again, if you live like no one lives now, you can live like no one lives later.

Once you've got it engrained in you that a growing savings account is your grubstake – your key to unlocking the matrix cell you've been living in – you will begin to spend less, save more and set your sites on the entirely possible goal of emancipation.

When you have saved enough for a big down payment on a house, you have attained your initial grubstake. Better yet if you can buy that first house for cash. But unless you were born to money, chances are you will have to finance that first house.

When you do, set it up so that you can pay it off as soon as possible – at the most, five years. If you can't do it in five years, I would say you can't afford the house.

Keep renting and save some more money. If you finance any longer than that you are back in the debt cycle for too long a term to ever make a clean break.

Make sure you have a clause in the contract for deed that states that you can pay off the contract early and without penalty. Banks would rather you didn't do this, since they make their money on interest payments. Make a conscious attempt to do just that. We had a five-year loan on our first place and paid it off in less than one year.

Again, look for cheap rundown property with good bones to buy. Do the required cosmetic improvements, spend elbow grease instead of capital, and plan on moving in a couple years, once you are exempt from paying capital gains on the sale.

In the meantime, pay down that mortgage as fast as you can. Remember, if you pay it off completely, every penny of the selling price of that house goes into your pocket. Your grubstake just got a whole lot bigger. And you may be able to pay cash for the next house.

Lather, rinse and repeat until you are both financially set and have found that dream place you want to live for the rest of your life.

Incidentally, I do realize that all of this moving would more difficult with children. But that doesn't mean it's not possible. I know people with children who have done it. And all that moving around has made their kids some of the happiest and smartest I know. Besides, when you do move, you don't necessarily have to move far.

Ironically and karmically, once you start down this road of investing in, fixing up and selling distressed real estate, it will be the banksters who will begin paying your ticket out of the darkness of their matrix.

Chapter 9

# The Power of Compound Interest

Every high school in this country should teach a required course on how to save money and, more importantly, regarding the power of compound interest.

And every parent should teach their children these same two things.

The trouble is that most parents nowadays are themselves unaware of the power of compound interest. This entire generation of parents and especially grandparents has largely bought into the matrix-controlled "get-rich" stock market scam at one level or another.

Many have taken a very cold bath. Some have taken several. And still, many cling to some fantasy that they too will be a millionaire someday if they just keep their head low and play by the matrix rules. It defies logic, not to mention indicates a moral bankruptcy unprecedented in humanity's span of time on this planet.

The seminal event in the downgrading of the concept of savings in the US came with the Reagan Administration's introduction of the 401K plan. This essentially privatized the retirement pension programs that most companies used to offer their employees for FREE.

The new 401K system was marketed as the best new thing since sliced bread. It sounded great since your employer would match your contributions to this stock exchange-based roulette scheme dollar for dollar.

What in fact had actually happened was that *you* were now matching your employer's contribution to your retirement plan dollar for dollar, essentially taking that corporation off the hook for the other 50% of your retirement that it *used* to pay.

Thank you very much sir, may I have another?

Worse yet, that previously stable and secure pension fund that nearly every American used to be able to count on in their old age was tossed onto the roulette wheel of derivatives, hedge funds and dark pools. Free from these billions in pension liabilities, for a while the Dow Jones went straight up.

Some who retired a few years ago were able to ride the up escalator and retire millionaires. But that once-in-a-generation aberration has since turned into another bloodbath for the masses, most of whom saw their retirement savings flushed away when the various bankster-conjured bubbles, with names like Internet, NASDAQ and Housing, burst and came crashing to earth.

A handful of *Illuminati* banks own 90% of *every* company listed on a stock exchange. They buy low and sell high – to YOU. You are extremely naïve if you believe otherwise.

I was lucky to be burned early by these lunatics, and my losses were minimal. Ever since, I have taken a much safer and simpler approach to the retirement we are already enjoying.

We buy Certificates of Deposit (CDs) offering the highest interest rates available in the US. And our rate of return in most years beats the pants out of that which we could get by investing in stocks.

You can find the best CD rates in the country online at Bank Rate Monitor and various other sites. We are currently going through a rough patch for savers, with record-low interest rates, but this won't last forever.

Luckily, I locked in two five-year CDs paying 5.25% and 5.26% APY respectively in 2008. Both banks get a 5-star CAMEL rating, meaning on a scale of 1-5, they are also considered to be two of the safest banks in the country. This is important.

Never invest your money in a bank that gets less than 3 stars on this scale. Try to stick with only those that get a 4 or 5-star rating. If a bank collapses, you will get your FDIC-insured money up to $125,000 per person or $250,000 per couple. Never keep more than these amounts in any one bank. Even so, it could take years to get *all* your money back from an insolvent bank, so stick to buying CDs at only the very safest ones.

In addition to that, buying a CD costs nothing. There are no brokerage fees and no capital gains tax when you cash it out. In normal economic times I prefer one-year CDs, since usually a better interest rate has come along by the time that year is up. But I guessed right that interest rates would go steadily down in 2008 and locked in the above rates for five years.

In the recent past I've gotten as high as 7% on a one-year CD. Nowadays even 5% is unheard of, but that will change.

Other than the lack of nickel-and-dime matrix fees and the fact that my CDs have easily outperformed the S&P 500 over the last 20 years; the other thing people miss about buying CDs is the difference between the interest you are now *paying* on a mortgage, a car, or whatever, and the interest you are *being paid* on a savings account or CD.

Assuming principle amounts to be equal, let's say you have a car loan at 4% and a mortgage at 5% and no savings or CD. You're down 9% to the matrix.

If you tighten your belt, pay off that car loan and buy even a 2% CD, you are now down only 3% to the matrix, since you still owe 5% on your mortgage, but have a 2% offset from the CD.

Now let's say you tighten your belt even more and pay off your mortgage. You now have the matrix in hock to *you* at a 2% annual clip. Pretty cool!

My wife and I now live almost completely off the interest paid to us by the banksters from CDs. To me there is something incredibly revolutionary about this. Imagine if everyone could be a creditor to these scoundrels, instead of a debtor. What a different world we would live in.

Once you have the bankers paying you to live, the power equation *vis-à-vis* the matrix, shifts in a fundamental way. You no longer have to bite your tongue at some slave wage job which services your debt. Self-censorship (the worst kind) can end in your life once and for all.

You can quit your meaningless job and take up something that really matters to you in this world. You can cease to define yourself according to your job. What matters to me is growing food, writing, travel and political activism. What matters to you will be different.

I really do believe that everyone has a calling in life. It's just that too many remained trapped in the matrix and never have the time to realize that higher purpose. With Americans working longer hours than ever, and husband and wife both now trapped in the matrix cubical, this has never been more true.

Computers were supposed to make things easier so we could all work less, right? Instead, these tracking devices enslave us even more to matrix central command structure, speed up our lives and consume even more of our precious time.

Economic liberation is the key to starting down a life path that has meaning. Once you have that grubstake earning you a regular income from the matrix banksters, you truly are on the road to living your dreams.

Chapter 10

# Get Back to the Garden

Everyone has their own dreams and it is for you and your family to decide how you want to live those dreams once you've got the banker paying your way.

But I must strongly suggest moving to the countryside.

There are many reasons to do this, not the least of which is that living in the country makes it much easier to avoid the entrapments of the matrix and further distance yourself from its tentacles.

Urbanization could well be the most dangerous trend on the planet. Cities are designed by the matrix, for the matrix and of the matrix.

I can't tell you how many times I've visited different countries and witnessed the misery and plight of the urban poor in sharp contrast to the lives of happiness and relative ease I've seen among the rural poor in those same developing nations.

It's the same here in the Ozarks.

Country folk here were decades ago disparagingly labeled "hillbillies" by the East Coast matrix press, mostly because they lived lives of incredible freedom and wore their stubborn independence from and defiance towards the system as a badge of honor. The great thing about the Ozarks, which in my view sets it apart from any other place I've lived, is that this rebel mentality is still alive and kicking in a palpable way.

City life is designed by the *Illuminati* lunatics to extract the maximum toll from each member of the middle and lower classes, for the maximum benefit of the ruling classes. If you live in a city, you are a cash cow to be milked daily by these sick fucks.

It starts with expensive property. You can't afford it. Nor do you want it. Many who bought into the suburban housing boom now find themselves living in ghost neighborhoods, unable to sell the house that is now worth half what they paid for it. Do you think that was just another coincidence?

Then there are the corporate factories and office towers, which city dwellers subsidize in all manner of underhanded ways while also being enslaved by one these welfare piggy facilities.

When they are released each day from their daily milking shift, they are not so subtly nudged by the nightly TV programmers towards a matrix-owned shopping mall, amusement park or restaurant where they are taught to be relieved of their grubstake under the guise of "rewarding yourself".

Then there is the crime, the traffic, the noise, the nasty recycled sewage you call city water and the air pollution. Worst of all is the mean-spirited attitude you will get from most all of the other imprisoned wage slaves.

Soon you will internalize this attitude yourself, becoming hardened, cynical and bitter. What Pink Floyd called, "alcohol soft middle age" is sure to follow. You will learn to hate the people and love the system. This in turn reinforces the matrix.

What you need, man, and you need it bad, is a return to living in the natural world. Where we live there is very little crime and – even better – very few cops. Our well water is sweet, our air is pristine and I can't see or hear my neighbors. It is very quiet. At night, when I go to sleep, it is very dark.

Most importantly, since we only go to town once a week, we don't have as many opportunities to internalize the insecurity and meanness of the majority of city folk. This makes it much easier to love the people and hate the system, instead of the other way around.

With nature constantly around us, we can tune in again to a thousand centuries-old human condition of being immersed in and part of the natural world.

When I do go to town, I can bring this renewed energy with me and try to help heal emotionally wounded city-dwellers with some positive and kind natural vibes.

The matrix is built primarily of consciousness. If we all changed our worldviews tomorrow to a "Love of Life" philosophy, the matrix would disappear by tomorrow evening.

Conversely, if we submit to its servitude, its cynicism and its general meanness, the matrix is reinforced, resulting in more war, more famine, more disease, more confusion, and less happiness.

This truism is why I believe we need a massive de-urbanization movement worldwide. If people continue to gravitate towards cities – to leave the garden – we will surely destroy this planet and we will never be liberated from the matrix.

Around the turn of the 19$^{th}$ century the vast majority (85-90%) of Americans still lived on a farm. Two centuries later only a tiny percentage (2%) still resided in rural areas

That's pretty serious stuff. And it's going on all over the planet.

To make a long story short, the matrix has stolen our land – robbed us of our birthright. Land is the economic base that everyone needs in order to become a producer rather than a debtor/consumer.

Once you own land in the country, you can begin implementing your plan for even greater independence from the matrix.

You can garden, plant fruit and nut trees, raise livestock and hunt and forage for wild edibles. You don't need a huge acreage to accomplish these things. You'd be amazed what can be done on just a couple acres. And remember, the bigger the acreage, the more there is to maintain.

Wooded acreage won't fetch as high a price as tillable land, so you can buy it cheaper. It's easier to maintain, and provides shade, shelter and habitat for all kinds of critters including you. Wood is also essential for free heat in winter time.

Look for areas where property values are reasonable, environmental pollution is minimal and property taxes are low. There are pockets of real estate which fit these criteria all across the country, depending on your climate and cultural preferences.

A good place to start your property search is online at United Country Real Estate's website. This company specializes in rural acreages and has offices in every state in the country.

Do a nationwide search after typing in your parameters and you will begin to see which parts of the country generally have the cheapest rural real estate.

Once you have identified these potential areas, you can research a few different places and see what they offer in terms of quality of life.

Once you decide on an area, you can view the full repertoire of properties for sale by switching to a broader multiple listing service (MLS) database for that specific area. Two good ones for the Ozarks are the Arkansas Multilist and the Missouri Multilist.

Once you have a base in the country you will feel even more empowered to "stick it to the matrix". Land is power. It provides an economic base from which you can produce things and create your very own systems.

As a political activist, I became very frustrated living in the city because I was always wanting to tear the whole system down, but was never able to use my creativity to *build* something.

When we relocated to rural America over 20 years ago, I felt more balanced. I still wanted to tear down the matrix, but I was now empowered to build our own, more just, parallel system to replace it with.

Interestingly this was the basic disagreement that Mao Tse Dong had with Marxism. Where Marx believed that the working class revolution would start in the urban factories, Mao foresaw that it would be spearheaded instead by rural peasants and farmers.

Historically, Mao has been right.

You may decide, as we have, to move several times, due to economic circumstances or because you just want to check over that next hill. Don't worry, once you have attained the skill set required to live in the country, you can remake entire systems at your new place.

Too many homesteaders dig into one place and commence with trying to buy their way to self-sufficiency. This is a big mistake. You'll burn through your grubstake on those expensive solar panels and be headed back to some meaningless job in no time.

It's not the stuff or even the particular place that counts. It's the *primitive knowledge* of how to survive and thrive in the country that matters. Once you start down this road to learning these skills, move around all you want. It's like riding a bike.

You'll become much more instinctive, which is the natural condition of humanity before the matrix got a hold of us. In this state, you become tuned into nature. Nature is revolutionary, changing constantly and hard to predict for the matrix logicians.

Once aligned with nature, you become a dangerous revolutionary to the system. And you have a piece of land from which you can righteously defend yourself, if need be.

The whole liberal argument that "we should never own land because the Indians didn't" is complete bullshit, probably planted into the discussion – as much "politically correct" nonsense was – by the matrix slaveholders.

First of all, just because Indians didn't have a "deed" to their land, doesn't mean they didn't most emphatically own it. Ask a Cree invader what the Lakota thought about him trespassing on their Little Missouri hunting grounds. Anthropologists call this "territoriality", but it comes down to semantics because the Lakota surely believed that land was theirs to utilize.

Second, times have changed, so adapt and quit seeking out ways to be a victim – the liberal scourge – for these assholes.

Once on your land, you can raise some livestock alongside that garden. You'll get good meat for your freezer or some goat's milk or eggs every morning, or some high-nitrogen manure for your garden, or all of the above.

If you raise a couple cows or pigs, you can sell one to a conscientious neighbor or friend and make enough to pay for the livestock and the feed, making your meat free. Try to grass feed your critters for the most part to keep your costs down. The good thing about pigs is they will eat almost anything.

If you could still use some cash flow, plant a high-value cash crop such as ginseng or shitake mushrooms. Or raise a few animals for the sale barn. Become a producer.

The key is to keep your equipment expenses down. Most all people in the modern age are enamored with machine power. What they fail to recognize is how expensive these are to operate and maintain.

You'll be amazed what can be done with a wheelbarrow, a shovel, a rake, a hammer and a couple good hand saws. Less moving parts require less maintenance and repair. Keep it simple.

Don't buy into any of the "end of the world" hype and buy a bunch of nutriciousless overpriced freeze dried food, ten generators or a missile silo apartment. All of this hype is designed to separate you from your hard-earned grubstake. Get to work and create your own systems for pennies. Then you'll be ready for whatever comes your way.

Lastly, look after your soul. When you reach a point where the banker is paying you enough to live without need, quit trying to make money.

Though you paradoxically need that initial grubstake to get free from the matrix, remember that money was never the goal in and of itself. Money is a Ponzi scheme that the matrix conjured up. The goal of attaining a grubstake is freedom and liberation from this matrix.

If you keep pushing on making more money when you already have enough, your mind becomes imprisoned, your soul hardens and you are right back at it helping to reinforce the matrix. Knowing when to quit worrying about making more money is very important. Only then you can really start living your dream.

Good luck!

# ABOUT THE AUTHOR

 Dean Henderson is a world-renowned political analyst, historian, and author of seven books, including his best-seller, *Big Oil & Their Bankers in the Persian Gulf.* Among the early truth-tellers to be ghosted and deplatformed by social media giants like Facebook and Twitter, Dean's Left Hook blog had millions of views when it was deleted by the NSA in 2014 and again in 2019. Despite decades of threats and harassment, Henderson has never wavered from his life-long commitment to revealing the evils of the worldwide oligarchy.

Raised on a multi-generational farm in South Dakota, Dean's politics were influenced by the Farm Crisis in the 80s and a trip to war-torn Nicaragua with Witness for Peace in 1985. He earned a Bachelors degree from the University of South Dakota and a Masters Degree from the University of Montana, where he began writing as a columnist for the *Montana Kaimin* and married his wife Jill.

A rebel from an early age, Dean took part in many political and social actions during his college days, summing up his views with hard raucous jabs at the reigning oligarchy of the day in his radical "zine", *The Missoula Paper.* In 2004, Dean won the Democratic primary for Congress in Missouri's 8th District and a year later published his first book, *Big Oil & Their Bankers...*

In 2018, he delivered a speech entitled *All Roads Lead to the City of London* as part of the Confronting Oligarchy: Resisting Full Spectrum Dominance panel at the Deep Truth Conference in New York City.

Over the course of his 30-year career, Dean's work has been published in hundreds of print and online magazines and websites including *Multinational Monitor*, *In These Times*, *Paranoia*, *Info Wars*, Save the Males.ca, Global Research.ca, Zero Hedge, Naked Capitalism, Rense Radio, Tactical Talk with Zain Khan, The Richie Allen Show, David Icke's Ickonic, Press TV, RT News, Russia Channel 1, The Syria Times. His books have been translated into German, Russian and Turkish.

# OTHER BOOKS BY DEAN HENDERSON

## BIG OIL & THEIR BANKERS IN THE PERSIAN GULF
### Four Horsemen, Eight Families and Their Global Intelligence, Narcotics and Terror Network

Big Oil exposes a centuries-old cabal of global oligarchs who control the global economy through manipulation of the world's central banks and control of the planet's three most valuable commodities: oil, guns and drugs.

## THE GRATEFUL UNRICH
### Revolution in 50 Countries

Henderson's travelogue asks the hard social, political, and economic questions as he discovers himself, humanity and revolutionary politics through meeting God's chosen people.

## THE FEDERAL RESERVE CARTEL

A well-documented history of the privately-held US central bank which is largely controlled by eight families.

## ILLUMINATI AGENDA 21
### The Luciferian Plan to Destroy Creation

Co-written with his wife Jill Henderson, Illuminati Agenda 21 follows the destructive trail of Luciferian hegemony from ancient Sumeria to the City of London which threatens to strip us of our humanity, replace us with machines and destroy Creation through technology.

# OTHER BOOKS BY DEAN HENDERSON

## NEPHILIM CROWN 5G APOCALYPSE

Nephilim Crown 5G Apocalypse is an indictment of the computer revolution as the latest mechanism through which royal bloodline families seek to control humanity. Since their intervention in Sumeria, these hybrid fallen angel Nephilim have usurped, steered, and plundered all of Creation as self-appointed god kings. The coming 5G apocalypse represents a great unveiling of not only their nefarious 5G deception, but of the fraudulent Nephilim Crown itself.

## ROYAL BLOODLINE WETIKO
## & THE GREAT REMEMBERING

Royal Bloodline Wetiko & The Great Remembering delves into the history of the royal Annunaki bloodline, which arrived in Sumeria around 8,500 years ago. The Cree word wetico means "cannibal of the flesh and soul". Henderson tracks this savage bloodline from Sumeria through Babylon, Egypt, and Rome to their current power base in the City of London. More importantly, he deconstructs the methodology used by this Crown to keep humans enslaved and isolated during this relatively brief period of human history. Drawing upon ancient Lakota culture to remind us who we are, Henderson sees a great remembering unfolding which makes this royal bloodline very nervous.

Made in the USA
Monee, IL
25 October 2023

45228323R00044